she is
Awakened

Awaken Your God-Given Calling,
Unleash Your Spiritual Gifts, and
Step Boldly into a Mission-Driven Faith
that Transforms Lives...
Starting with Yours

www.ChristianBusinessResources.com

Title: She Is Awakened

ISBN: 978-1-917815-14-7

Category: Spiritual / Business / Christianity

Foreword by LaWanna Bradford, MPA

*Best-selling Author, Speaker, Entrepreneur,
Strategist, and Transformational Leader.*

she is Awakened

Awaken Your God-Given Calling,
Unleash Your Spiritual Gifts, and
Step Boldly into a Mission-Driven Faith
that Transforms Lives...
Starting with Yours

www.ChristianBusinessResources.com

Foreword

Your divine call to rise, remember, and respond to who God created you to be.

I was thirteen years old when I gave my life to Christ.

At that age, I did not yet understand theology or doctrine. What I did understand was fear. If I am honest, I was scared into the Kingdom. Something in me long before I knew what 'FOMO' was carried a deep fear of missing out. Missing out on God. Missing out on eternal life. Missing out on belonging to Him.

So, one day, with trembling hands and a pounding heart, I whispered yes to Jesus.

It was not a sophisticated decision. It was not polished or poetic. It was the raw, fearful, awkward "yes" of a girl who desperately wanted to make sure she did not miss the Kingdom.

And yet, that yes has been the most powerful decision of my life. Because here is the beautiful truth: God honors even our trembling yes. He takes what little we bring, breathes His Spirit upon it, and transforms it into destiny.

From that one scared yes, He has written a story with my life that I could never have imagined. That shy girl uncertain of her place, unsure of her worth grew into a woman who has travelled the world, encountered cultures and people of every kind, and stepped into spaces of leadership and entrepreneurship that demanded courage I did not know I had.

Through it all, one unshakable truth has anchored me: my relationship with Christ is the source of my strength, my leadership, and my ability to love.

More Than One Dimension

I often tell people: we are not one-dimensional.

Yes, we have minds. Yes, we have bodies. But we are not simply our thoughts, and we are not merely our flesh. These are the vessels, the vehicles through which we experience time and space.

At our core, we are Spirit. Eternal. Divine image-bearers of God. And when we awaken to that truth when we align with our divine essence through the Holy Spirit, we see the world differently. We see ourselves differently. We realize we are joint heirs with Christ. We understand the creative power entrusted to us by God. We grasp that we are not walking blindly through life but guided by the Spirit who orders our steps according to the Word.

This awareness awakens us. It transforms how we live, how we lead, and how we love.

And that is what this book is about: awakening.

Awakening as a Lifestyle

Awakening is not a one-time event. It is not a single moment of goosebumps at an altar. Awakening is a lifestyle. It is the continual choice to lift our eyes above fear, distraction, and doubt, and to align with the One who wrote our story before the foundations of the world. Awakening is hearing His voice and responding with a steady, daily yes. This book is your invitation to that lifestyle. It is your divine call to rise, remember, and respond to who God created you to be. And the journey begins here.

So, let's look ahead to what you will find throughout the pages of *She Is Awakened.*

Made for Miracles – *Su Park*

Su's chapter reminds us in Made for Miracles that life with God is not meant to be ordinary. We are called to live with Kingdom expectancy. To believe that Heaven can touch Earth in our daily lives. To release miracles not as rare exceptions but as the natural outflow of faith and obedience.

The early Church lived this way. They prayed, and the ground shook. They believed, and the blind saw. They obeyed, and entire cities turned to Christ. That was not history, it was a blueprint. Su's chapter is a bold reminder: you were made for miracles.

Dreaming with God – *Courtney Carlson*

Courtney takes us deeper in Dreaming with God. Awakening is not just about what God wants to do in you, it is about what He wants to do through you. And He does not do it alone. He invites you to dream with Him.

Think about that: the Creator of the universe, the Author of history, says, "Let us dream together." He deposits visions that are bigger than you, ideas that stretch nations, dreams that restore broken hearts. Courtney's chapter is a stirring call to co-create with God, to step into visions that shake the world awake.

Drenched in Destiny – *Michelle Mckown-Campbell*

Michelle reminds us in Drenched in Destiny, that destiny is not abstract it is daily. It is not just a far-off future; it is the purpose you live every morning when your feet hit the ground.

Walking in destiny means owning your God-designed identity and authority. It means living drenched not dabbling in the calling God has placed on your life. And when you do, confusion falls away, and clarity rises.

Heaven's Voice, Her Yes – *Clare Fuller*

Then comes the tender yet fierce voice of Clare Fuller in Heaven's Voice, Her Yes. Every awakening leads to a question: Will you say yes?

Yes, when the Spirit whispers. Yes, when obedience feels costly. Yes, when the world says no. Clare's chapter calls us to the kind of obedience that doesn't just hear but responds. Because transformation doesn't happen in theory - it happens in obedience.

Fuelled by Faith – *Willetta Carson*

In Fuelled by Faith, Willetta brings fire. Awakening without faith fizzles. Faith is the fuel that crushes fear, ignites courage, and builds unshakable resilience. This is not passive faith. This is active, mountain-moving, fear-dismantling, atmosphere-shifting faith.

Faith is what turns trembling yeses into world-changing testimonies. Willetta's words will remind you: faith doesn't just sustain; you were created to be fuelled by it.

Anointed for Impact – *Vanessa Frater-Robertson*

Vanessa moves us from faith to activation in Anointed for Impact. Every gift God placed inside you was meant to be used. Not buried. Not hidden. Not hoarded.

The anointing on your life is not for you alone it's for the marketplace, the mission, the people waiting on the other side of your obedience. Vanessa's chapter will awaken dormant gifts and remind you: you are not ordinary. You are anointed.

Holy Spirit Strategy – *Sammy Garrity*

Sammy takes us into divine strategy in Holy Spirit Strategy. Strategy that doesn't come from textbooks but from Heaven. Wisdom that defies logic. Clarity that pierces confusion.

When Sammy and her husband Greg gave their lives to Jesus in 2023, they stepped out like Abraham, selling their home, giving away possessions, and moving to Texas with nothing but radical faith. Out of that refining season, God birthed Kingdom Catalysts, a ministry equipping men and women to walk in faith and become change agents.

Sammy's story is proof: when God says "Go," obedience always unlocks strategy.

Courage Over Comfort – *Desiree Parsons*

Desiree reminds us in Courage Over Comfort that awakening will always require a choice: will you cling to safety or step into boldness?

Silence may feel safer, but it costs too much. Comfort may feel secure, but it kills destiny. Desiree's words will embolden you to roar with Heaven's voice, to choose courage over comfort, and to step into the kind of bold faith that shakes atmospheres.

Birthing Kingdom Ideas – *Michelle Watson*

Michelle shows us in Birthing Kingdom Ideas that awakening births more than courage, it births creativity. Kingdom ideas are not just good ideas; they are divine blueprints meant to shift culture and catalyse change.

Michelle will guide you into stewarding those ideas, nurturing them, and releasing them into the world. Because the Kingdom is not only proclaimed - it is built.

Equipped to Reign – *Angel Theodore*

Angel continues the building in Equipped to Reign. Leadership in the Kingdom looks different. It is not about domination but about love. It is not about control but about liberation.

To reign is to serve with authority, to love with power, and to lead with Christ at the center. Angel's chapter is a call to become the woman who doesn't just survive but reigns, because she knows Whose she is.

Commissioned and Unstoppable – *Drocella Mugorewera*

And then comes the crescendo: Commissioned and Unstoppable by Drocella. Awakening is not just personal, it is missional. You are not just awakened to feel inspired; you are awakened to be sent. To be commissioned. To be unstoppable.

Drocella's chapter is a commissioning moment, a charge to rise as a Kingdom catalyst, a daughter on divine mission.

My Heart for This Book

I would be remiss if I did not share why this foreword is so personal for me.

I first got to know Sammy Garrity, the leading catalyst of this book, many years ago through her Global Ripple Makers Movement, before she ever gave her life to Christ. Back then, she was already a force of nature, inspiring, equipping, and empowering people to step up as catalysts of change. What I see so clearly now is that God was at work in her all along. Even before she knew Him, He was preparing her, shaping her, and using her gifts to help others bring their impact to the world.

Since giving her life to Jesus in July 2023, it has been one of the greatest joys of my life to see her step into her true calling. The journey has not always been easy, but it has been beautiful. I have loved watching her grow in faith, leaning on God more and more, and realizing that everything she was doing before was simply preparation for this Kingdom Catalysts Ministry assignment.

When she and her husband Greg first surrendered, they did not have all the answers. They didn't even know where God was taking them. But by the end of November 2023, when God kept giving them the same word, they went all in. I watched in awe as they gave away most of their belongings, sold their home on the water, and with nothing but pure faith, flew to Texas with their three dogs and two cats to live in the Bible belt. No safety net, no plan B, just a burning desire to follow Jesus completely.

A month later, they opened their first Bibles. When they read about Abraham, the "Father of Faith," who simply went when God said, "Go," they saw themselves in his story. They too had stepped out in faith without knowing what was ahead, but with complete trust that God would lead the way. That has been their posture ever since: when God says go, they go, and He has been faithful to them every step of the way – as you'll see in Sammy's chapter about Holy Spirit Strategy.

In Texas, God refined Sammy and Greg. He stripped back the old and made way for the new. Out of that refining came Kingdom Catalysts –

the ministry they are now building to equip men and women all over the world to walk in faith and become catalysts of change in their own families, communities, companies, churches, and even nations.

I have seen firsthand how God has transformed their lives, and I know this: Sammy and Greg are living proof that He can use anyone. We think we need to have it all together, but we do not. All we need is to give it to the One who holds it all together.

That is why it was such an honor for me to be asked to write this foreword. Because this is not just another book, it is God sharing His heart through each of the authors and their testimonies of what He can do through you when you surrender everything.

I pray as you turn these pages, you'll be stirred to believe for more, to live with radical faith, and to step boldly into the calling God has placed on your life.

A Prayer Over You

Heavenly Father,

We lift every reader of this book before You. Thank You for awakening her spirit, reminding her of her divine identity, and calling her to respond with bold faith.

We declare that she will rise in love, authority, and courage. That fear will not hold her, doubt will not silence her, and distraction will not derail her.

Holy Spirit, order her steps according to Your Word. Surround her with Kingdom mentors. Align her with divine assignments. Ignite in her a fire that cannot be quenched.

"Lord, release miracles, dreams, destiny, faith, boldness, and divine ideas over her life as she reads each chapter. May she not only be inspired but transformed by Your healing love and redeeming grace.

In Jesus' name, Amen.

With love and blessings,

LaWanna Bradford

About LaWanna

LaWanna Bradford, MPA is a best-selling author, speaker, serial entrepreneur, strategist, and transformational leader with more than 30 years of impact in finance, leadership, and innovation. She is the creator of The R3 System™, a framework that empowers leaders to Refocus, Reframe, and Reconnect to turn disruption into opportunity. As COO of The Bradford Group, she has uncovered and implemented more than $2 billion in efficiencies for corporations and government agencies.

She is also the author of I Pledge Allegiance: A Journey Through the Words That Shaped a Nation, and a sought-after speaker on leadership, faith, and transformation. Her life's work is to help people rise into their divine calling with courage, clarity, and conviction.

Learn more at: www.LaWannaBradford.com

Connect with LaWanna:

Facebook: www.facebook.com/lawanna.bradford.3

Instagram: www.instagram.com/thelawannabradford

LinkedIn: www.linkedin.com/in/lawannabradford

Get your free gift on how to live successfully with the R3 System™ — Refocus, Reframe, and Reconnect. at: https://linktr.ee/Lawannabradford

Dedication

This book is lovingly dedicated to all our sisters in Christ.

To the sister who has questioned her worth.

To the sister who has carried her calling alone.

To the sister who has been told she is "too much" or "not enough".

To the sister who is tired, weary, or wondering if God still sees her.

Sister, He sees you. He has never left you nor forsaken you. And you were born for such a time as this. We dedicate this book to every daughter of the King who is ready to rise, shine, and awaken to her true identity. You are not forgotten. You are not disqualified. You are anointed, appointed, and deeply loved by God.

May every page remind you of the truth you've always carried in your spirit... you are chosen, you are equipped, and you are unstoppable when you walk with Him.

This book is our offering to you. Because God has a heart for women, and so do we

With love and blessings,
Your She is Awakened sisters xx

Contents

To subscribe to the worship songs playlist, where you will find all of the songs listed throughout this book, visit:

https://www.youtube.com/
playlist?list=PL7ZkC7sTOyS6zL3p9VAtyiSTvgLrNaSuh

Introduction

Dear Sister, welcome to She is Awakened. This book was written with you in mind.

It is more than the words you will find on the pages inside. It is a global movement, a calling, a reminder of who God created you to be, and an invitation to be part of the story as we grow the Kingdom Women Catalysts ministry.

Over the last year we have spoken with hundreds of Christian women, and our hearts broke as we listened. Time and again, we heard the same themes: isolation, exhaustion, fear, and even the temptation to quit. Women who were called by God, filled with vision, and burning with purpose, yet carrying their assignment alone and feeling invisible in a world that often misunderstands faith. That is why this book exists, because you are not alone. And because your voice, your gifts, and your calling matter in the Kingdom.

We are believing for a mighty move of God through the lives of 100,000+ Christian women who are ready to prosper with purpose, be fuelled by fire, and filled with faith, so that collectively we can pour the fruits of our successes back in to our families, communities, churches, ministries and worldwide causes.

We hope that you will join us as we build it together.

Inside these pages you are going to meet eleven women leaders who share their raw, personal stories of the trials and triumphs they have faced on their Christian journey. They write not as women who have it all figured out, but as women who said "yes" to God and discovered the miracles, strength, and strategy that come when you walk in step with the Holy Spirit

Each chapter is filled with encouragement and practical tools to help you awaken your identity, unleash your faith, and step boldly into your divine purpose.

This book also marks the launch of a global women's ministry, Kingdom Women Catalysts. Together, we are believing for a revival: a global movement of women rising as catalysts of change to shine our light brighter together than we can alone.

And because this is bigger than us, 100% of the proceeds from this book will go directly to Global Renewal, a ministry dedicated to rescuing, restoring, and empowering women and children from cycles of exploitation and abuse. Their work is an extension of the very heartbeat of this book: to awaken women to their true worth, their freedom, and their God-given future. You can learn more about this fantastic cause at: www.globalrenewal.org

This is your time. This is your awakening. And we are so honored to walk this journey with you.

With love and blessings,
Your She is Awakened sisters xx

Chapter One

MADE FOR

Miracles

How to live with Kingdom expectancy and release Heaven on Earth through faith and obedience.

I grew up in a very anti-Christian family, forbidden to go to church or even say the word God. My parents made it clear that the Christian faith was not welcome in our home. I remember my sister-in-law, who was a believer, once told me, "Su, I believe God can do the impossible, but your mom and dad coming to Christ? Impossible. They will never believe in Jesus." But God had other plans.

After decades of prayer and declaring His promises, I saw the miracle I had been waiting for. Acts 16:31 says, "Believe in the Lord Jesus Christ, and you will be saved, you and your household." I clung to that verse with everything I had. And guess what? My mom gave her life to Christ at age seventy-seven, in church, in front of our senior pastor and many witnesses. My dad followed at the age of eighty-four.

What looked absolutely impossible to man was never impossible to God. Even my own salvation was a miracle. For most of my life, I believed I would die if I ever set foot in a church. That's how much fear and resistance had gripped me. And yet, here I am today, a living, breathing miracle.

Searching for Meaning

As the youngest of seven, I was loved and spoiled. At my school in Memphis, Tennessee, I was popular and accepted, even though I was one of only two Asian students there. On the outside, it looked like I had everything. But inside, something was missing. I was searching for meaning but I felt trapped. I knew if I went near a church, my parents would kill me. I grew up believing it was dangerous to even explore faith. Yet God already knew me.

For years, I resisted. When someone once told me that I was a sinner, I was offended. "I don't steal. I don't kill. I might lie, but I'm not a sinner." I was spiritually blind to my need for grace. Then one day, while I was driving down the freeway, it happened. Something hit me, not physically, but spiritually. Out of nowhere, I broke down in tears. I cried and prayed, asking God to forgive me. In that moment, I saw the truth: I was a sinner in need of forgiveness. I surrendered my life to Jesus Christ.

That encounter with the Holy Spirit changed everything. The King of Kings came down to reveal Himself to me - a girl full of sin and pride. That's the greatest miracle of all. From that moment, I was never the same.

2 Corinthians 5:17 says, "If anyone is in Christ, he is a new creation; the old has gone, the new has come." That became my story. I am living proof. The old me, blinded, self-centered, trying to live life my own way, that girl is gone. In her place stands a new creation, filled with the Spirit of God.

Since then, I have witnessed miracle after miracle. God has healed people before my eyes, provided in times of need, opened doors I didn't know existed, and transformed hundreds of lives before me. But I no longer see miracles as rare or surprising. They are part of who God is – and because I am His daughter and made in His image - they are part of me too. Before the foundation of the world, God knew us. He fearfully and wonderfully made us. He calls us His masterpiece.
That in itself, is a miracle!

Living With Kingdom Expectancy

So many people are shocked when they see God perform a miracle. But we shouldn't be. Miracles are the natural culture of the Kingdom. The world says, "That's impossible." But heaven says, "With God, all things are possible." We don't live by the limitations of this world. As children of God, we have access to heaven's resources. We carry His DNA. And because of that, we should expect miracles as part of daily life.

When I became a Christian, I used to hope God might move. Now, I live with the expectation that He will. This shift came through faith, through learning to trust His Word above my feelings, reasonings, and above what my eyes could see.

> *"Now faith is the substance of things hoped for, the evidence of things not seen." - Hebrews 11:1*
> *It's trusting the heart of God when your circumstances make no sense.*

My turning point was when I realized my human reasoning could never fully understand God's ways. He is limitless. He is the God of galaxies, of all time, of eternity. I am just a created being. My job is not to figure Him out, it's to trust Him to figure it out. And I learned that His Word is always true.

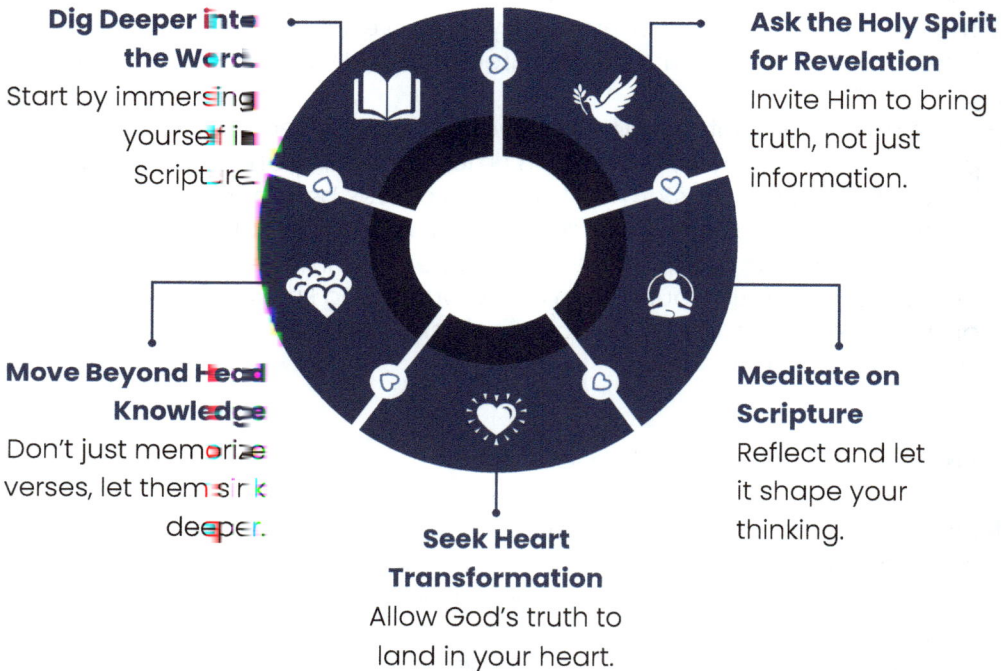

Dig Deeper into the Word
Start by immersing yourself in Scripture

Ask the Holy Spirit for Revelation
Invite Him to bring truth, not just information.

Move Beyond Head Knowledge
Don't just memorize verses, let them sink deeper.

Meditate on Scripture
Reflect and let it shape your thinking.

Seek Heart Transformation
Allow God's truth to land in your heart.

If you want to increase your faith, begin with digging deeper into the Word. You can know Scripture in your head, but head knowledge puffs up, it doesn't change your heart. I know so many people who can quote verses and yet they don't feel it in their hearts. You have to move beyond intellectual knowledge to revelation, God's truth landing in your heart. That comes through meditating on Scripture and asking the Holy Spirit for revelation, not just information.

And when you feel doubt rising, know that it isn't from God. The enemy feeds lies into our minds and he's very good at it. If you don't know what God really says about who you are, you'll swallow those lies and be driven into fear, anxiety, and worry. Those things are not the fruit of the Spirit. So, you must learn to recognise the enemy's voice.

How? By knowing God's voice first, knowing who God says you are, and what you are entitled to as His daughter. If you don't know that, you can't win in life.

Renewing your mind is non-negotiable. Thousands of thoughts run through your head each day; you must filter them. Ask: Is this thought coming from God, or from the enemy? Everything God says aligns with His character, He is loving, caring, affirming. He will never shame you. Jesus took our shame and guilt on the cross. Yet many Christians live under shame and guilt because they're listening to the wrong voice which empowers the enemy. Faith is an active process.
"We demolish arguments and every pretension that sets itself up against the knowledge of God, and we take captive every thought to make it obedient to Christ." 2 Corinthians 10:5

There Are Miracles in Your Mouth!

Remember Zechariah? An angel told him that he and his wife would have a child in old age, and he doubted. Because of his doubt, God closed his mouth until the promise was fulfilled. Words matter. God created the universe by speaking. As His children who carry His DNA, our words have creative power. Proverbs 18:21 says "Death and life are in the power of the tongue, and those who love it will eat its fruit." When we speak God's truth, we give it permission to manifest.

Say, "I am healed," don't just think it.
Declare, "I am restored," don't just wish it.

When you verbalize the truth of Scripture over your life - healing, provision, freedom - you are releasing the miracle. It is not magic; it is exercising the authority Jesus gave us to trample the works of the enemy.

I encourage you to also change the way you pray. God already knows your needs - He's omniscient. We are not beggars; we are His children seated at the table, and He invited us to sit there. So, stop begging and start thanking God as if you have already received what you are asking for: "Thank You, Father, for my healing. Thank You for my provision. Thank You for my family's salvation."

Thanksgiving is a declaration of faith; it shifts your heart and aligns your words with God's will. Faith without action is dead. Faith that is only comfortable, convenient, or contemplative does not move heaven. God has given you everything you need. He is waiting on you to step out and act in faith.

If you are fighting fear or illness, stop rehearsing the bad report. Stop quoting the medical chart as if that is your final word. Change your speech. Let the weak say, "I am strong." Declare your identity in Christ – speak healing, restoration, abundance and freedom over yourself and your household. The miracle often lives in your mouth first. Believe with your heart and confess with your mouth. That combination silences doubt and builds a faith that expects miracles as a part of everyday Kingdom life!

> *A verse that helps me stay aligned with God every day is found in John 15:5: "I am the vine; you are the branches. If you remain in me and I in you, you will bear much fruit; apart from me you can do nothing."*

This truth has become my anchor. God is with us 24/7, and I know that I cannot live or do anything without Him. The question is not whether or not He is available, but if we are. Alignment is about my willingness to remain connected, through relationship, not religion. Religion says, "Do this, don't do that." Relationship says, "Come close, know Me, and let Me love you."

God gave us free will. He could have made us robots who automatically obey Him, but He wanted sons and daughters who chose Him out of love. That means every day I have a choice of how I spend my time, where I set my mind, and who I let influence my heart.

For me, it starts every morning. Before I do anything else, I set time apart for Him, to worship, read His Word, and listen. I talk with Him throughout the day too, but carve out focused time every morning and evening where I can pour out my heart and hear what He's saying. This way of life truly helps me to live victoriously and witness His miracles.

Jesus said the greatest commandment is to love God with all your heart, soul, mind, and strength, and second is to love others as yourself. But how can you truly love God if you don't spend time with Him? Think about marriage: you don't commit your life to someone you hardly know. You spend time together, you build trust, you grow in intimacy, and you know each other's voices. That's what a daily relationship with God is like.

One of the biggest lessons I've learned is that there's nothing I can do to make God love me more, and nothing I can do to make Him love me less. Romans 5:8 says, "While we were still sinners, Christ died for us." That means His love is already settled. My role is simply to remain in Him.

I don't want to be a "submarine Christian," hidden all week, surfacing only on Sunday mornings. God calls us to shine His light daily, so others are drawn to Christ through us. That requires consistency, not just occasional connection.

Of course, trials and unexpected challenges still come, start taking them as a compliment. Sometimes they mean you're a threat to the enemy. The enemy attacks to discourage, but God has already given you authority in Christ. Luke 10:19 says, "I have given you authority to trample on snakes and scorpions and to overcome all the power of the enemy."

Walking in that authority takes daily surrender and obedience. Sometimes God's instruction is simple - open your Bible, encourage someone, or take one step of faith. Other times, it is bigger. Recently, He told me to start a prophetic evangelism team, not just to share my faith, but also to equip others to step out of their comfort zones. That's what alignment looks like: being available, listening, and obeying.

And here is the beautiful part: when you abide, when you stay connected to God – you begin to see miracles. Not one-off events, but an overflow of living in relationship with a miracle-working God. Jesus Himself said we would do even greater works than He did. That is not you striving, it is Christ in you. All He asks is that you remain, stay available, and step out in faith.

Living with Kingdom Expectancy

Maybe you've wondered, "Why does it seem like miracles are for other people, but not for me?" I want to tell you something today, if God did it for them, He will do it for you. He doesn't play favorites.

> **Ephesians 3:20 reminds us: "Never doubt God's mighty power to work in you and accomplish all this. He will achieve infinitely more than your greatest request, your most unbelievable dream, and exceed your wildest imagination. He will outdo them all, for His miraculous power constantly energizes you."**

His love for you is so vast, as wide as the ocean. It never runs out, it never runs dry, and it is available to you right now.

That promise is not just for a chosen few. It is for you, your family, your ministry, your heart and all the more - for every area of your life. His Kingdom resources are available to every single child of God. You are not a second-class citizen in His Kingdom. You are chosen, loved, and worthy.

One of the best ways to build unshakable faith is to study the miracles of God from Genesis to Revelation. The more you read them, the more faith will rise in you. Every miracle is evidence of His power, and every testimony is an invitation for Him to do it again in your life.

And please don't fall into the trap of comparison. God showed me this so clearly while I was snorkelling in Aruba. I was surrounded by thousands of colourful fish, all unique in design. Not one of them fought for space. They each thrived exactly as God created them. The same is true for you – there is more than enough of His love, His presence, and His miracles for every single one of His children. You don't need to compare yourself, you simply need to live in the presence of God and thrive in the way He designed you.

So today, stop waiting for "someday." Stop watching other people step into their miracles and start stepping into your own. God has already given you the "go." Your time is now!

Your Action Step

Take time each day to study the miracles of Jesus in the Gospels.

Choose one or two that stir your heart.

Then write your own declaration of thanksgiving around it.

Speak it daily, and watch not only your faith rise, but miracles too!

Here are some scriptures for you to meditate on as you pray about being made for miracles:

> *"I have been crucified with Christ; it is no longer I who live, but Christ lives in me; and the life I now live in the body, I live by faith in the Son of God, who loved me and gave himself for me." Galatians 2:20 NIV*
>
> *"When you live a life of abandoned love, surrendered before the awe of God, here's what you'll experience: Abundant life. Continual protection. And complete satisfaction!" Proverbs 19:23 TPT*

Here is a prayer-filled declaration to expect miracles every day of your life:

Heavenly father, I declare that I am fearfully and wonderfully made in Your image, and that You are the God of miracles!

You love me and adore me perfectly, unconditionally, and eternally. I am highly favored by You, God, and Your people.

I declare miracles are happening all around me and I praise You daily for Your supernatural interventions and provisions. I have access to all heavenly resources and I can use them any time as needed.

I declare I have been activated with the resurrection power of You God, as Christ lives in me and I in Him. I walk by faith, and I obey You cheerfully.

God, Your goodness, mercies and blessings follow me all the days of my life.

I declare in Jesus' name that I shine Your light brightly wherever I go because I am anointed and full of You, God. I am blessed to be fruitful, multiply, fill the earth, and take dominion. I'm the carrier of heaven on earth and I love expanding Your kingdom.

I declare according to 1 John 4:4 that GREATER is He that is in me than he that is in the world! Today, I declare I will see Your miracles, God, as I open my heart and mind to receive Your Word, which helps me to see all things through Your heavenly perspective.

Today I declare that I am like God, I think like God, and I do life the way God intended me to live. I thank You father for this abundant life of freedom and victory.

In Jesus name I pray, Amen.

Some worship songs to help you own your God-given identity and purpose:

1. New Thing Coming by *Elevation Worship* (feat. Tiffany Hudson & Steven Furtick)

2. God of Impossible by *Lincoln Brewster*

3. Here Comes the Kingdom by *Jake Fretz*

4. Another One by *Elevation Worship (feat. Chris Brown)*

About Su:

The Family, Faith, & Freedom Coach, Su Park,
is a seasoned family coach with over 30 years of
experience helping families transform through
biblical wisdom and practical strategies.
As a certified Kingdom parenting and life coach,
Su has dedicated her life to equipping, encouraging,
and empowering families to thrive, with a special
focus on church leaders, couples, parents, and young adults.

Having served as a children's pastor and family ministry director for
27 years, Su has impacted thousands of lives by nurturing a love for God
and a foundation of faith-based principles. Her work with the National
Center for Biblical Parenting has taken her across the nation,
where she's inspired and equipped families in seminars focused on
biblical parenting that led to healing and restoration.

Rooted in her own journey of finding faith and purpose,
Su's coaching approach is deeply compassionate and uniquely
insightful. For those seeking meaningful change, Su provides a trusted
path to discovering purpose, freedom, and abundant life with lasting joy.

For more information or to connect with Su Visit www.suparkcoaching.com.

Connect with Su on...

Facebook
www.facebook.com/su.suhpark

LinkedIn
www.linkedin.com/in/suparkofficial

Instagram
www.instagram.com/susuhpark

Chapter Two

DREAMING

With God

How to co-create your powerful Kingdom vision with God.

Have you ever wondered what the Lord has planned for you?
Women, like you and I, spend time dreaming of what our lives would
look like. But have you ever wondered what God dreamt for your life?
Before life's circumstances shaped you with worries, doubts, trauma,
pain, and unbelief. Lately, I've realized that my dreams are good,
but God's are even better. It's hard to fathom that God had plans for us
from the beginning of time, before the foundation of the earth.
He knew what lay ahead of us and still calls us good.

I couldn't imagine a love like this. A love that was and is so radical.
Even now the depths, and the weight of this hit me. Not just the surface
level, but the weight comes from the depths of knowing God had a plan,
He has a plan, and He will work it out all for good. For your good and
mine. I wondered deep down if God could really do something through me.
I wanted to believe but I knew myself. I knew that I was nothing special.

> **At an event recently, a speaker said "Your flesh is bad,
> my flesh is bad, get over it. God can do more through
> you than you could even imagine".**

That struck me. I have a lot of faith. I believe that God can move
mountains because I've seen mountains move, bodies healed and more.
Yet my low self-esteem often held me back. I kept seeing myself through
the lens of my flesh, through failure and sin, rather than through the Spirit.
I was missing the big picture. Maybe you have felt that way too?

The truth is it's God through us. It's in our Spirit man that God's power is
on the move. Our old man, the fleshly man is dead and gone. We are
made new by the redeeming of our mind and believing what God says
about us. Putting on the mind of Christ requires you to be bold.
Bold enough to believe what God says about you. That's a scary place
to be, isn't it? Sometimes we believe it in part, but the moment life gets
hard, or someone doesn't see what we see, we throw it all away.

We don't realize that we can stand in the power of God every moment of every day.

Right now, I want you to take a moment and invite God into every part of your life and day. Ask Him to breathe His life into you and into your circumstances. Invite Him to show you how He sees you and what He wants for your life. Let Him dismantle any religious Spirit and step into your teacher or guide. Let Him love you back to life. I know, because I have done it many times. Each time He invites me into this place I am redeemed and made new. I feel the weight lift from my shoulders. It's not about my image but His. Not my strength, but His. He is the One who makes us new. God's dreams for your life are so good. But you may be wondering: *How do I move forward when people or circumstances are still holding me back?*

God's dreams for your life are so good. Believe me, I understand. For me, the greatest hindrance was self-hatred. I didn't like who I thought God had made me to be. I disliked my personality, my quirks, my ways. I spent years dimming my light, withholding my full capacity, and sabotaging my progress. I hid the real me because I feared rejection. Maybe you do this too?

I couldn't live the life I wanted to live believing these lies. I had to release them in order to step into my purpose and calling. I discovered that dependence on God has to be tangible. I read about this family with courageous faith. God asks them to sell their house and after they do, with nowhere to go, they sit down on the front steps. At that moment, a friend calls and says that he is donating an airplane! God was taking their ministry on the road. Talk about down to the wire and living out your faith. God, I wanted faith like that! Do you have faith like this? Do you want faith like this? Our dependence on God in the little things and huge steps is key. We need to seek God in all things. Listen until He responds then take the steps He tells us to take.

I have ADHD and dyslexia therefore learning has always been difficult for me. I desired to learn scripture and I asked God "where do I begin?" He led me to Jeremiah 29:11. It was as if He was saying, "Courtney, my plans for you are good. I won't hurt you or leave you in pain" and He hasn't. I've faced some painful, scary moments but God has fulfilled His promises in me. He is faithful and knows what He is doing. Through wisdom, healing and equipping, God led me to the life that I lead, tangibly. The life that He wanted me to lead all along. Words can't express the healing and growth He has given me.

For what was once a broken, hurting little girl, is now a thriving wonderfully loved woman, mother, teacher and friend. God's plan for your life is deeper than you could ever imagine. More powerful than we deserve and full of more goodness than we can handle. As you reach for your dreams with the Lord, allow Him to guide you to new levels of freedom and life. Allow the self-hatred to fall off of you and step into this new season, changed and full of Holy wisdom from heaven.

Activation
Take some quiet time with God today and begin to dream with Him.

Find a quiet space. Bring your Bible, journal and a pen.

Pray: Ask God, "Show me how You see me. Show me the dreams You had for me before the world got hold of me. Show me what you want me to do next."

Write without filtering. Write down any images, words, impressions, or scriptures that come to your heart. Don't overthink it, just let it flow.

Ask Him again: "God, what part of myself or my past do I need to release in order to walk into Your dream for me?" Note what He reveals.

Declare truth: Out loud, thank God for His good plans for you. Speak Jeremiah 29:11 over yourself: "God, your plans for me are good. I receive them today."

Take one small step. Choose one action you can take this week that aligns with what God showed you.

Remember: You're never dreaming alone; you are co-creating with the one true God who restores hearts and shakes nations. You've got this!

With love, Courtney.

A scripture for you to meditate on as you dream with God:

"For I know the plans I have for you," declares the LORD, "plans to prosper you and not to harm you, plans to give you hope and a future."
Jeremiah 29:11 NIV

A prayer to help you dream with God & co-create your powerful Kingdom vision:

Lord, grip my heart for what grips yours. Send me to the places you'd want me to go. Let my life be a sign, a symbol and a testimony of your Glory, your goodness, of your redemptive love and power.

Lord, I thank you that you are so tangible in our lives. That you see my suffering yet won't leave me there. You step in to be with me. You miraculously save us from our pain, our past, from ourselves. You take us where only you can. Where no man gets to go without you. To a successful life, dreaming, and playing with you. Let us all feel chosen, known, loved, provided for and taken care of by your love.

Lord, you are my testimony and reason for being. I love you with all my heart. Continue to grip my heart for what grips yours.

Amen.

Some worship songs to help you dream with God:

1. Goodness of God, Bethel Music *by Jen Johnson*

2. You Came, Bethel Music *by Jonathan David & Melissa Helser*

3. Find Me, Bethel Music *by Jonathan David & Melissa Helser*

4. I Surrender *by Hillsong Worship*

About Courtney:

Courtney is a Christian author, speaker, and transformational coach who offers practical breakthrough tools through her workbooks and video courses, 'Self Discovery' and 'Intimacy with God' available on her website. Courtney's coaching approach centers on self-awareness, radical honesty, and deepening your intimacy with God, helping you experience real emotional healing and spiritual breakthroughs.

For travel dates to an event near you check out Courtney's website and stay in touch. Visit www.the-colorful-table.com and join her newsletter.
.

Connect with Courtney on...

Facebook
www.facebook.com/courtney.carlson.938925

LinkedIn
www.linkedin.com/in/courtney-carlson-colorful-table

TikTok
www.tiktok.com/@courtney.carlson18

Gift link
www.the-colorful-table.com/
booksandresources/p/free-self-discovery-pdf

Chapter Three

DRENCHED

In Destiny

How to discover what it means to walk daily in your God-designed purpose and authority.

Let me be real with you. I didn't walk into this journey with God with grace. I came kicking and screaming.

There's a part of me that knows deep down that I'm exactly where I'm meant to be. But then there's my head, full of old programming, fear, and doubt, telling me to run, to play small, to go back to what's safe and continue to believe that I am on this journey alone.

Perhaps you know that feeling too.

Maybe, like me, you've felt like you were too far gone. Too messy. Too complicated. Maybe you've carried shame so heavy that the idea of walking in any kind of purpose feels impossible. Wondering, could God really love someone like me?

For a long time, I used to joke that if I ever walked into a church, I'd be struck by lightning. But it was no joke, because I truly believed this. I thought too much had happened; I'd been away for too long for Him to love me. I could see the lightning, and I could hear it crashing all around me. But that niggle to return never left me.

Through the years, I have returned. But as welcoming as people were, it wasn't long before I had talked myself out of attending, heading straight back to where I had come from. Not because I didn't believe in something bigger. Oh, I believed! But because I didn't believe I belonged there. Throughout all the years, I never stopped talking to Him, being guided by Him. Being loved by Him. If only I had realized this.

This feeling of not belonging isn't new to me. It's a feeling I have felt deep within my soul from the beginning of time.

You see, when people hear me on the phone, they assume I'm white. I have a well-spoken southern English accent. But I'm Anglo-Caribbean. My mum is White English. My dad is Black Jamaican. My caramel skin tells a different story, and when people meet me in person, I see it: the pause, the confusion, the question: "Are you Michelle?" And since moving from the UK to the USA, I see it even more as people assume I am African American or, as someone said once, Latino. You can imagine their surprise when I speak.

I've seen those looks and heard the whispers all my life. From the pram lying next to my twin brother, who had blond afro hair and lighter skin, and me, darker with jet black hair. All my life, I have heard the murmurs, the questions, and seen the looks of people trying to work out who belonged to whom. Even now, with my own family, I still see the looks.

As a teenager, I was consumed with understanding how I fit in this world. Not being able to answer this question for myself, I started to believe that I just didn't belong. Which, over time, somehow transitioned into me believing I was so invisible that if I left this world, no one would notice. There was no reason at the time that led to this, no trauma or experience that anyone would have been aware of. I had friends and was doing ok at school. I was passionate about dance and music. I was just a normal teenage girl.

Nobody knew what was going on inside my head because I didn't understand it. I couldn't describe it, and so I couldn't speak to anyone about what I was experiencing. But little by little, it consumed me until it (the darkness) had fully taken over. I had all the proof that I was not meant to be in this world. For me, the proof was everywhere.

At the age of 15, I believed with absolute certainty that if I were to leave this world, I would not be missed. I believed I was so invisible that no one would notice I had left. So, I made the biggest decision of my life. To go, for good. There was no doubt. Nothing to discuss.

I remember sitting on the floor in my bedroom at boarding school. I sat comfortably and quietly speaking to Him. Tears streamed down my face. I remember being surrounded by absolute peace and calm. It felt so right. I felt safe, and I was ready.

My roommate came into the room where I was sitting and, without even noticing me, looked for something, sighed, and left. That was all the proof I needed in that moment. The proof that YES, I was invisible, and it was time to leave.

Time stood still. There was no noise at all. Taking a deep breath in, fully in the knowledge that I was at peace. I was ready to say goodbye forever. But that day in that moment, in the middle of the silence, that friend shouted up the stairs, "MICHELLE!!!!!!! Do you know where my black shoes are?" She shouted it as if this was not the first time she was asking, and that tiny, ordinary question interrupted everything.

It snapped me out of the spiral like a thunderbolt.

In that moment, I was pulled back from the dark straight into the light. I was pulled suddenly back into the world I was trying to escape from.

To this day, I don't think she knows what she interrupted. That moment saved my life.

But the shame and guilt of being in that place never ever left me. From that moment on, it shaped how I moved in the world. How I let others treat me. How I saw myself. And how far I believed I was from God.

That disconnection ran deep, into everything.

The truth? I didn't realize how dark my world had become. That's the thing about it. It happens slowly and silently. Without realising it, you are just going through the motions. Life looks "fine" from the outside. But inside, bit by bit, the colour fades. One shade at a time, until, before you know it, you are fully in the dark. Or worse than that, living in the grey.

I knew what it felt like to be fully in the dark. I knew after that I didn't want to go there ever again. So, I did everything I thought I needed to do to move myself towards the light. I spent years trying to earn love by partying, drinking, and performing. I was wild and loud on the outside, but I was lost and scared on the inside. I crossed lines. I got hurt. I did all of this because I wanted to fit in and I wanted to belong, even if it broke me more.

What blows my mind is that my name is Michelle, and had I tried to explain how I was feeling back then, I would have said that I felt as if I was in 'my shell'. Peering out from inside. Sitting right at the back of it, in the dark, comfortable in the shadows. It took me many years to realize that I was not afraid of failure. I knew what that felt like. I also knew what it felt like to just do enough, to get by, and live in the grey. What I was terrified of was being in the light. Fully in the light, knowing who I was and knowing I was not alone because God was by my side, and He loved me just as I was.

I was comfortable and uncomfortable all at once, but more trapped and stuck than I ever knew. I was desperately seeking to bring the colour back into my life. I thought I needed to find that through others. Filled with shame, guilt, and remorse about what I was doing, I retreated into the shadows, back into 'my shell'. If only I had known, then what I know now.

What I know now is that without light, you can't see your dreams.

Without seeing the light, color, and vibrancy in ourselves, we can't feel and see the beauty surrounding us. We live life at a distance. Separated as if there is a vast space between us and the world. Sometimes even now, I find myself crawling back into that shell, and I must remind myself to gather the proof of my tapestry of awesome to bring the color back into my world.

But that's where I was.

In 'My shell.' I believed I was too far from God, without purpose, believing that there was no way back.

Moving to the United States changed everything. As soon as my feet touched North Carolina soil, my world went BOOM!!!! I just knew I was here for a reason. After all the excitement of the move, what happened next was totally unexpected. Because of my visa, I wasn't allowed to work. I couldn't even volunteer because no one could do a background check on me. For three and a half years, I returned to the shadows where I had to sit with myself. With the silence and with the question: Who am I? What do I want to do? Why am I here?

Slowly...

In the stillness...

In the questions...

I began to hear His voice as He guided me to do the work I was meant to do. Crazy thing was, it was work that I had done all my life. I was being called to start a business and stand in the light fully. It was so scary because what was being asked of me was never on a vision board. Over the years, I had often ranted about why people did not see their awesomeness. Why did they not connect with their full potential? Why!!" On this day, though, as I ranted, I heard Him answer. "Because you have not started to do the work." That's when I realized this was God's purpose for me.

Throughout my 25 years in HR and in my work as a Transformational Speaker and Reengagement Strategist, I have seen firsthand that too many people are living in the grey without even realising it, and that's why I started my business and created Activate the Awesome®
It's not just keynotes, workshops, and a framework.

It's about first Discovering the (A.W.E) - God

(S.O) You can Connect with Holy Spirit, already inside each of us.

And become Inspired (M.E) Jesus

Or as I now call them, my spiritual team.

It's about reengaging with your sacred identity, knowing that YES, you are worthy. YES, you belong and YES, you fit in. Just as you are.

Not because I have told you. But because you have gathered the undeniable proof of your awesomeness. The good. The messy. The incredible. The broken. All of it is part of your tapestry of awesome. All of it is proof. All of it belongs.

Doing this work has been my bridge back to faith.

That was how I began to recognize the miraculous.

How my business came to life.

I now know that it was born through God!

For years, I called God the Universe. I was so grateful to the Universe, Source. But it is God, it is Jesus, it is the Holy Spirit. It was always my spiritual team. He never left me. They never left me They always loved me??? or is He correct?? I think they, as I am referring to my spiritual team.

Now, before I open my eyes in the morning, I talk to the Trinity, my Spiritual Team. All through the day, I share and thank them. They are my team. They are my light. They fill me with joy and love. I know with them I can do all things.

I remember kicking and screaming at the beginning of this journey and asking, "How can I surrender fully to something I don't understand?"
The answer came back softly: "Start from where you are.
Time will provide the answers." And that's exactly what I've done.

So, if you've ever felt too broken, too far gone, too unsure.
Please know that you are not.

You are not alone. Your spiritual team is with you.

You are seen.

You are known.

You belong.

You are loved.

And they walk beside you.

One of the activities I get my Activate the Awesome® clients to do is create a prayer wall. It is a simple, practical exercise that will help you to fill yourself with His light, start a real conversation with God, and make honest prayers visible so you can receive forgiveness, guidance, and assurance. Let's do this together now.

Prepare a Space

Find a quiet corner with a journal and pen. Light a candle or add something that reminds you of God's presence.
A sacred space will help you focus and expect Him to meet you.

Fill Yourself with His Light

Close your eyes, breathe deeply, and pray: "God, fill me with Your light." Picture His light surrounding you, pushing out fear. Allow His presence to replace fear with peace.

Speak Honestly

Talk to God out loud, as you would a trusted friend.
Share what's really in your heart, hopes, struggles, or fears.
Faith begins when you're real with Him.

Write Your Prayer

On a card or page, write:
- Date / Title
- My request
- Why it matters
- What I release/confess
- A scripture (optional)
- One step I'll take this week

Writing makes your prayers clear and memorable, not just to God but to you, too.

Create Your Prayer Wall

Place your card somewhere visible. Make sections for "Prayers" "Waiting" and "Answered." Seeing prayers reminds you to believe and expect answers.

Revisit with Gratitude

Return often to read, pray, and listen. Move answered prayers to the "Answered" section and thank God out loud. Gratitude strengthens your faith.

Keep the Conversation Going
Add new prayers, update old ones, and reflect on what God is showing you. Faith grows through building up an ongoing dialogue with Him.

Always remember You are God's masterpiece, drenched in destiny, crafted with purpose, crowned with authority, and called to shine. No shadow, no past mistake, and no voice of doubt can erase the destiny He has written over your life. When you choose to step out of the grey and walk drenched in His light, as I did, you don't just discover your purpose, you ignite it. So, rise with boldness, walk with confidence, and live knowing you were designed for impact, for love, and for such a time as this.

A scripture for you to meditate on:
"For we are God's masterpiece. He has created us anew in Christ Jesus, so we can do the good things He planned for us long ago." – Ephesians 2:10

A prayer to help you walk daily in your God-designed purpose and authority:
"Lord, thank You for calling me out of the dark and into Your light. Help me to walk daily in the purpose You designed for me. Amen."

Worship songs to help you own your God-given identity and purpose:

Jireh *by Elevation Worship & Maverick City*

Who You Say I am *by Hillsong Workship*

Graves into Gardens *by Brandon Lake*

Waymaker *by Michael W. Smith and Vanessa Campagna*

Light of the World *by Lauren Daigle*

About Michelle:

With over 25 years of experience in HR, recruitment, coaching, and leadership development, Michelle Mckown-Campbell is a Transformational Speaker and Re-engagement Strategist, inspiring leaders, teams, and individuals to reconnect with their God-given identity and purpose. As the creator of the Activate the A.W.E.S.O.M.E.® framework and one of the first Global Positive Impact Mapping® Practitioners, Michelle has already served thousands of people across organisations, schools, and communities, helping them awaken confidence, elevate strengths, and unlock potential.

Her vision is bold: to **Activate the Awesome® of one million people by 2034.** Through transformational keynotes, creative workshops, and interactive experiences, she equips people of all ages to rediscover their value, re-engage with purpose, and shine brighter than ever.

Michelle doesn't just speak - she activates. Every person she reaches is invited to gather the undeniable proof that they matter and are uniquely designed for impact.

For more information about Michelle and the programs she delivers at Activate the A.W.E.S.O.M.E.®,

Visit:
www.activatetheawesome.com

LinkedIn
https://www.linkedin.com/in/michellemckowncampbell

Chapter Four

HEAVENS VOICE,

Her Yes.

How to lean into the work of the Holy Spirit with heart obedience.

What does it all mean? Why am I here? What is the point of me? What purpose do I have?

Why do I feel so alone even though I'm surrounded by people?

What is wrong with me? Why do I feel like I'm never enough, and yet feel too much at the same time?

I don't understand, why am I even here?

The questions swirled like a storm in my mind, relentless and unyielding. The weight of them pressed against my chest, making it hard to breathe. I sat by my bedroom window, daylight filtering through, but the light could not reach me.

The darkness was closing in, wrapping around me like a suffocating fog. Would it not be better if I were gone?

Tears blurred my vision as I cried out in pain to God.

"Lord, why am I here?"

My voice was barely a whisper, yet my soul was screaming. Why did You create me, only to let me suffer so much pain? So much darkness?"

I needed Him to answer me. I needed Him to tell me I mattered. I knew I couldn't leave, for my family's sake. But why did I have to stay?

And then, in the suffocating silence, something shifted. A presence.

In my mind's eye, a fine, glistening thread appeared - like a spider's web, delicate yet unbreakable - stretching from my heart into the darkness. It shimmered, defying the void. And then I heard a voice, deep within me:

"No matter how far away I seem, I have you. I will never let you fall. Give it all to Me, for My yoke is easy, and My burden is light."

A thread of grace. A tether to the One who had never let me go.

That night, as sleep began to embrace me, I experienced something like a vivid dream. My eyes were shut, yet I was awake, aware of the bed beneath me and the bedding wrapping around me. I was back in that place - the place where my innocence was stolen.

But this time, He was there.

Jesus.

He stepped into the memory, His presence overwhelming the pain. I saw Him lift me up as a loving father lifts his little girl - strong, protective, safe. He held me tightly, His arms shielding me. Then He spoke:

"I take away all the sins that were done to you. I take away all the sins you have done because of the sins that were done to you. I make you clean."

I wept. My body shook, the weight of years of shame, guilt, and self-hatred breaking, cracking. I opened my eyes, tears still streaming down my face, and for the next few days, I could not stop singing:

Amazing grace – "My chains are gone; I've been set free..."

A Moment of Clarity

That Sunday at church, I saw my sons with their friends - 16 and 18 standing tall and strong. Across the room, I noticed a group of young girls between the ages of 12 and 13, giggling and whispering to each other. In that instant, something shattered inside me. I saw the stark contrast of the young girl's vulnerability next to the strength of the young men. How could it ever have been my fault?

At 52 years old, after 40 years in the wilderness, the veil started to lift, and light shone on the truth. The shame, the guilt, the burden of believing I was bad to my core started to soften. My long-held belief that if there was a God, I was unlovable in His eyes, began to slowly fall away. For the first time, I caught glimpses of myself through His eyes, and my heart received the truth: I was fully known and still fully loved.

The traumas I carried, He had known them all. And slowly, one by one, He met me in each of them. He walked me through the surrendering of the pain, the suffering, the heartache, the shame and the guilt.
And in exchange, He gave me something lighter.

Who Am I?

It was only after this journey of surrender that a startling truth emerged, I didn't even know who I was. I had mastered the art of becoming whoever the moment required. Shapeshifting, moulding, bending myself into whoever other people wanted / expected / needed me to be, so they wouldn't see me as 'bad'. So much so, I had lost myself, or maybe I had never even found myself to lose her.

Have you ever felt this way?

For me, she was buried beneath the rubble of trauma, under the weight of other people's expectations, wants, desires.... trapped by fear. She had never known her own voice. Her own dreams remained whispers in the background of her life.

Like the first light of dawn touching the darkest corners of my heart, this realisation awakened something long forgotten or perhaps never found. And in the darkness, a question began to form that burned like fire in my soul.

Who am I? Who am I?

The question kept going around in my head, haunting me, circling in my mind like a relentless tide.

Who was I underneath all the traumas? Who did God create me to be?

And so, I decided to ask God Himself.

At the time I was reading through the Psalms. It was where God had led me after revealing to me that the abuse was not my fault.

Each morning, I read a Psalm, noting what it revealed about God's character, building a picture of who God is, and highlighting a lesson I felt was for me to embrace. Then I journalled, pouring out my heart to

Him using words from the Psalm to help me to express how I truly felt to the depths of my heart, surrendering it all.

And so, after journalling, I decided I would sit in silence and ask: Who am I, Lord? Who am I in Your eyes?

Eyes closed, heart open, I would listen for His response and whatever words or phrases came to me I wrote down. The answers were gentle, affirming - nothing like the self-hatred, torment and accusations I had hurled at myself for years.

Next, I asked Him; What are my gifts, Lord? What am I good at? The words came and again they were kind. I continued through each question I had and after several days, I sensed the Lord had given me who I was in His eyes

To my astonishment, when I later shared my reflections with a close friend, her answers mirrored what the Lord had shown me - affirming the truth He had placed in my heart.

Taking what I had been given, I began to mindfully sit with God and ask Him to show me my I AM statements. Who I am at my core. Not labels like "mother", "wife", "businesswoman", but the deepest truths of my being.

Slowly, twelve I AM statements emerged, twelve undeniable truths.

I never intended to have twelve, but when I looked down at my journal, that's what was there. And as I spoke them aloud, they settled within me like roots growing deep into the earth. For the first time, I stood on solid ground. And I knew that from this place, God would rebuild my life.

I was becoming.

A season of Surrender

As I continued to spend time with God, he gave me a new assignment: Create joy.

I sensed a new path was unfolding and that God was going to change me from the inside out, but it required my obedience to create joy in my life. This felt unfamiliar to me, so I knew I had to do something different. I decided that every time I noticed something didn't bring me joy, I would bring it to God, sit with Him and seek His understanding, His guidance of what needed to change so that joy could replace the weight of the darkness I felt.

Each time He showed me what needed to change. Sometimes it was my perspective, other times something within my own heart. Occasionally I needed to set a boundary or have a difficult conversation. There were moments when I had to shift the position someone held in my life. Through it all, He was right there alongside me, showing me the way, cracking my dislocated life back into place.

Then came the hardest change I needed to make; letting go of my business – the very thing that provided for my family. I wrestled with this decision, torn between fear and faith, but in the quiet moments God whispered, "Trust Me".

So, I did.

I told my husband I needed to release it. He encouraged me to sell it instead of closing it down, and miraculously, God made a way.

Then came His next assignment: Rest.

Rest? I had been working since I was 13. The idea was foreign. But moment by moment, He showed me how to be still, how to simply be. He taught me to live from my 'I AM' statements instead of constantly striving for the world's approval.

Nine months of surrender. Nine months of healing. Every time I tried to push ahead, He whispered: "Not until January."

The waiting felt endless. But then, January arrived, and suddenly, doors began to open. Pieces fell into place and Fuller Life™ was unfolding.

My Purpose, His Plan

Now, I understood. The trauma. The wilderness. The breaking. It was never about destruction. It was about transformation. Everything - every trauma, every excruciating moment of facing my past, every painful surrender - was preparing me.

I was meant to walk this path so I could lead others through their own darkness. So, I could show them how to heal, how to unearth their buried selves, how to step out from the crushing weight of fear, shame, guilt, and the lies they have believed.

My purpose was clear: Show others the way.

To show them how to heal from the traumas that bind them. To guide them in uncovering who they were created to be, buried beneath the rubble of pain, shame, and unworthiness. To remind them that their identity is not defined by this world - not by parents, peers, society, or their past. Only by the One who created them. By God, whose love is never failing, who is forever faithful and who never ever leaves us.

The world will tell you who you should be. It will pull you down an arduous, frightening, lonely path, twisting your identity to fit its mould.

But if you look inward - to the Spirit within you - and upward - to the God who fully knows you and fully loves you – then you will find your purpose, your truth.

Your I AM
Saying no to the world and yes to God takes courage. It requires strength, trust, surrender, and above all, a personal relationship with Him, for we cannot trust a God we do not know.

As I look back now, I regret that it took me 8 years after becoming a Christian, to dive into the Psalms and truly build a personal love relationship with Him.

And so, below is an invitation to go on a journey, to know who God truly is. Not through someone else's lens, but through His own words. Walk with me through the Psalms and beyond. Let's discover together the One who fully knows us... and still, fully loves us.

Because when we know Him and see Him as He truly is, surrender becomes possible. And in that surrender, we find our purpose. We find who He created us to be and discover freedom in the life we were always meant to live, a Fuller Life, fully free from the weight of this world.

Discovering Your "I Am" Statements

ACTIVITY: Discovering who God really is and who you are in Christ.

One of the most life-changing moments in my journey was discovering who God really is and how He sees me - who I am in Him. In doing so, I was able to trust Him, let Him heal me, and show me the path He has for my life.

Step 1: Create a quiet place
"Come with me by yourselves to a quiet place and get some rest" Mark 6:31 NIV

Create a comfortable, undisturbed space where you can be with God. Bring your Bible, journal, pen, and maybe some Bible highlighters. Take a few deep breaths, relax your shoulders, and quiet your mind.

Step 2: Prayer, invite God into this moment.
"But when you pray, go into your room, close the door, and pray to your Father who is unseen. Then your Father, who sees what is done in secret, will reward you". Matthew 6:6 NIV

Close your eyes and pray, inviting God into this moment. Ask Him to guide you as you seek Him and your identity in Him.

Step 3: Anchor in Scripture
We have this hope as an anchor for the soul, firm and secure. It enters the inner sanctuary behind the curtain"
Hebrews 6:19 NIV

Ask God to guide you to scripture that reveals who He is and who you are in Him. In my journey, it was the Psalms. Highlight or underline each word, phrase or the even the whole verse where God reveals who He is, teaches a lesson / gives instruction or makes promises. Do this each day until you begin to trust God and feel safe in His presence. Aim for at least 7 days if you are new to this.

Invitation: If you'd like to join me on a guided Journey Through the Psalms, **visit https://www.clarefuller.life/journey_through_the_psalms.** For each Psalm, you'll find a short video where I share what God revealed to me as I journeyed towards a personal love relationship with Him.

Along that journey, He led me to *Psalms Today,* a beautiful series by one of my church elders Peter Mead, where he shares one helpful tip for reading each Psalm effectively and one key detail to notice as you apply its truth to your life today. It's been such a blessing to me, and I've shared the link for each Psalm so you can enjoy it too.

Step 4: Reflect – Who Am I?

"For we are God's handiwork, created in Christ Jesus to do good works, which God prepared in advance for us to do". Ephesians 2:10 NIV

Once you know God and feel safe with Him, at the back of your journal, dedicate one page per Question:

- Who am I at my core, beneath all the roles I play and the expectations of others?
- What are the gifts, strengths, and passions God has given me?
- What am I naturally good at, and what brings me joy?
- When I look at my life through God's eyes, what truths emerge about my worth, identity, and purpose?

At the end of your Bible time, close your eyes, place your hand on your heart, focus on your love relationship with God and ask Him the first question. Write down every word, phrase, or image that comes to you. Don't over think it – just let His truth flow in and through you to the page. Do this for each question. Repeat daily for at least 7 days or until you think each question has been answered fully.

Step 5: Invite wise counsel

"Plans fail for lack of counsel, but with many advisers they succeed" Proverbs 15:22 NIV

Share the questions and your reflections with a trusted person – a friend, pastor, coach, or family member. Invite them to respond from the perspective of someone who knows you and encourage them to ask thoughtful questions that help you explore your answers more deeply and gain greater clarity.

Step 6: Form Your I AM Statements

"For you created my inmost being; you knit me together in my mother's womb. I praise you because I am fearfully and wonderfully made; your works are wonderful; I know that full well". Psalm 139:13-14

Using your answers and reflections, create your I AM statements. Truths about who you are, rooted in Scripture and God's Word.

For example:

- I am chosen and beloved

- I am enough, precious in Gods sight

- I am forgiven and belong

- I am safe and free in Christ

Aim for at least 3 statements. You can always build on them over time.

Step 7: Be your "I AM" daily

"Trust in the Lord with all your heart and lean not on your own understanding; in all your ways submit to Him, and He will make your paths straight". Proverbs 3:5-6 NIV

Keep these I AM statements somewhere visible - on your mirror, fridge, or phone. Speak them out loud each morning to root God's truth into your life.

Check in with your trusted person to see how you are living these truths, adjust as needed.

Rooted in your "I AM"
You will know your I AM statements are right when they bring peace, truth, and joy - and awaken the courage, boldness, and strength to live each day from who you are in Christ.

The healing begins with us, but it does not end with us. It transforms the next generation. Because Trauma doesn't get the last word, God does.

This is the heart of Fuller Life™. To build a global movement of passionate women transforming wounds into wisdom, pain into purpose, and healing into an awakening that echoes through generations.

A Prayer to Know God's Truth and Who He Created You to Be

Dear Father,

You are the One who fully knows me and still fully loves me. Help me to know who You are, show me Your truth, that I may know You not through the world's lens, but through Your own words.

As I draw closer to You, help me to uncover who I truly am in You and Your purpose for me.

Give me the courage to face the truth, the strength to release what was never mine to carry, and the faith to walk the path You have set before me. Shape me, refine me, and lead me into the fullness of who You created me to be.

May Your light break through every shadow, and may Your love be the foundation upon which I stand.

In Jesus name, with love, Amen x

Scriptures to Meditate on:
"Have I not commanded you? Be strong and courageous. Do not be afraid; do not be discouraged, for the Lord your God will be with you wherever you go." Joshua 1:9 NIV

"For I know the plans I have for you," declares the LORD, "plans to prosper you and not to harm you, plans to give you hope and a future. Then you will call on me and come and pray to me, and I will listen to you. You will seek me and find me when you seek me with all your heart." Jeremiah 29:11 NIV

Worship songs as you seek to hear His voice:
As you listen to the songs below, breathe in His presence. Let His voice whisper to your heart and guide you into the Fuller Life He lovingly prepared for you.

A quiet place: The Secret Place (acoustic)
by Phil Wickham, Madison Cunningham

For when you don't have the words.
Amen *by I Am They*

When you need reminding that God cares for you:
Who am I *by Casting Crowns*

It's time to own how much you are loved:
Belovedness *by Sarah Kroger*

Heal your heart, see through His eyes:
Hosanna *by Hillsong United*

About Clare:

Clare is a Somatic Trauma-Informed Leadership Coach, mentor, trainer and founder of Fuller Life™, a global movement of passionate women transforming wounds into wisdom, pain into purpose, and healing into an awakening that echoes through generations.

Having shaped her own story of Complex PTSD into a path of healing and purpose, Clare knows that true transformation requires both tenderness and strength. She's trained in Neuro Linguistic Programming, Brain-spotting and Silent Counselling, informed by Internal Family Systems and the Dynamics of Biblical Change. Her personal journey fuels a deep commitment to championing others as they step into lasting, meaningful change.

Clare walks alongside women with compassion, offering a safe space, practical tools and powerful strategies to help them gently uncover what clouds their path and heal deeply. She empowers them to embrace the fullness of who they were created to be, equipped to keep rising, healing and living in ever-deepening freedom.

For more information about Clare and her programs

Visit:
www.Clarefuller.life

Linktree:
https://linktr.ee/ClareFuller.Life

Chapter Five

FUELED

By Faith

How to Build Unshakable, Fiery Faith that Crushes Fear and Ignites Impact.

Did I ever tell you about the time I heard voices. Not voices in my mind but external voices. It was as if someone was standing next to my bed and whispering in my ear. The voices whispered, "love the devil. worship the devil." This happened every night and as sundown approached, I would get more and more nervous.

I was tired. I had barely slept for weeks as I was up most of the night because of the voices. If anybody had asked me if I was a Christian, I would have said yes. So, you can imagine both my anguish and my shame when I kept hearing this voice. The voice that whispered "Love the devil. Worship the devil."

It spoke simultaneously and independent of my own thoughts. I couldn't ignore it because I thought if I did, it meant I was agreeing with it. I spent the night fighting it. Pleadingly I would say "I don't believe that. That's not true. This is not me. I know this isn't me." But the voices wouldn't stop. It was torture. I didn't dare tell anyone for fear they would think I was crazy.

I would do things like recite the Lord's prayer, or one time I got the family Bible but I didn't know what to do with it. I even held my mother's rosary in my hand as though it would magically work against the voices like some kind of symbolic incantation, but nothing helped.

I got so desperate that I decided to talk about it, but indirectly. With rings under my eyes from lack of sleep, I would tell my mother, sisters and friends that evil thoughts kept coming into my mind. "Really bad thoughts," I said. I chose my words carefully because I was ashamed.

I had visions of them putting me into a mental hospital or thinking that I wanted to be a Satan worshiper. This went on for about two weeks and the last person I talked to was my dad. My father raised us to believe there wasn't anything he wouldn't do for us, and it was true. But even he couldn't help me this time.

That night I finally talked to God, and I talked to Him like a real person.

I said, "God, I know you are the only person who can help me!"
I cried out, "Please help me!"

In my desperation I looked up expecting Him to answer... and He did.

I wasn't surprised when He spoke. I was just so happy. His voice was also not in my mind but external. It was as if the air itself had spoken. He said, "Get the Bible." I leaped out of bed and grabbed the family Bible from the shelf. Immediately I started to think differently. Instead of asking him what page to turn to, I thought. "God knows which page I am going to turn to."

So, I just opened it and read whatever was before me. It was a children's story at the beginning of the Bible where the disciples wanted to stop the children from bothering Christ. For some reason when I was done the first thought that came to my mind was "I have to have faith." "I must have faith!" Then I looked up again with expectation and God's voice spoke one more time. He said, "Go to church tomorrow." Indeed, it was Saturday night but even more importantly I noticed for the first time since it had started that the voices were gone and the room was filled with a beautiful peace. That night I slept like a baby.

The next morning my mother woke up and said, "I don't know why but I feel like going to church today. Willetta, will you go with me?" You wouldn't believe it, but after all that had happened I shrugged my shoulders and said "No." I said that I didn't feel like it. It reminds me of that old saying *'How soon they forget'*.

God had delivered me, and I was grateful but quick to forget what he said that night. Then suddenly I remembered a dream that I had had the night before. In the dream both God and the devil were present, and they were discussing me. Right then, I knew that I had to go to church that morning.

When I agreed to go, my mother was so excited she behaved as though she had won the lottery. "Really?" she exclaimed. "Okay, okay, let's go. Let's go. We've got to hurry." It had been so many years since we had gone to church that we didn't even remember what time the service started, but we managed to get there just a few minutes before the service began.

When we got to church there was a visiting preacher. He was a young student in his twenties who had just finished seminary school at the University of Chicago. He looked very earnest as he stood at the front of the congregation in his suit and tie with his tufts of blond hair that hung just below his ears. He was nervous. He said he had been praying for weeks for God to tell him what he should talk about in his very first sermon and he finally got his answer last night. God told him to give his testimony on how he became saved. It was a before and after story about the incredible change in his life, but more importantly as his story unravelled everything he said, everything that happened to him, was as if he was talking about me.

He told stories of torture by evil forces and trying to get help but realized that only God could help him. The similarities were so uncanny that even my mother nudged me during the sermon and said, "That sounds just like you, Willetta." My mother was astounded. My eyes welled up with tears. I was in awe as I realized that the night before God told this young seminary graduate what to preach and sent me to hear it. God also knew that my 18-year-old self would be too fickle to go to church, so He put the desire in my mom's heart to go and for her to be a witness.

After church, I was elated! For the first time I realized that God saw me. He was interested in me. God Almighty did all of that just for me and that day was the beginning of my journey with God.

Later that fall I went away to college. Although I had been to church many times I had never heard of salvation or what it meant to truly be a Christian. So, after many students had witnessed to me about their journey with Christ, I was convinced that Jesus Christ had died on the cross for my sins. Someone had given me a tract about how to live a spirit filled life. So, I went back to my dorm room and with my free little Gideon bible, I re-read it and went through every scripture that had been given to check and see for myself what people had been telling me. You see, I believed that the Bible was the word of God, but I had never read it... not one page of it! But it was all there in black and white. It was true. So, I accepted Christ as my personal saviour, and I was set free. I was a new creation in God, and I have never looked back.

God taught me many lessons from that experience, but I have never forgotten that God told me I have to have faith! Faith in God has been the cornerstone of my life and my foundation. Through thick and thin, ups and downs, God has never let me down. Just like He talked to me that day, He is also talking to you. You may not hear His voice with your ears, but you can hear Him with your heart and that is what matters. God is saying. "I love you. I see you. I want a relationship with you. Believe in me. I am here for you."

The fear of God is the beginning of wisdom and believing in God is the beginning of faith.

My discovery can be your discovery too!

You can believe in something without having faith, but you cannot have faith without belief.

At the beginning of my journey I believed in God, but I didn't have faith. I believed in God enough to know I needed Him, but I didn't know that I could talk to Him or that He would listen. In my head I knew that I had exhausted all my options, but it was my heart that cried out to Him and in my desperation, I finally knew that He would answer. Knowing in my heart that God would answer was the beginning of my faith.

The faith God gave me through that season taught me to have faith in myself. It changed my life. It transformed me from the inside out, and I became the version of me that God had always meant me to be. From that moment on I wanted to help others get to know Him and experience all the love that I've experienced.

Through His unconditional love, God taught me to love myself and be empowered by that love to do anything through faith. It's this kind of fire-filled faith that I want to help you activate, because when you activate your faith, you can build a relationship with God that crushes fear and ignites the kind of purpose-filled impact that has the power to move any mountain in your life.

That is why I am building an empowering faith-building community called "Fuelled by Faith", where women can deepen their relationship with God, find their purpose and step fully into their calling.

Let's take some time now to get you started in turning your belief into fiery faith.

My breakthrough came the moment I cried out to God in desperation, expecting Him to respond, and He did. This activity will help you practice that same kind of faith-filled conversation with God.

Step 1: Write Down Your Fear or Struggle
On a piece of paper or in your journal, write down the fear, lie, or struggle that has been tormenting you. Be honest and specific.

Step 2: Declare Who God Is
Next to it, write down a truth or scripture about God that directly counters it. For example:

Fear: "I feel alone."
Truth: "God is with me always" (Joshua 1:9).

Step 3: Cry Out in Faith
Now, speak out loud to God, just as I did. Pray something like: "God, I know only You can help me. I trust You to speak to me and guide me right now."

Step 4: Expect to Hear His Voice
Sit in stillness and listen with your heart. Write down any word, phrase, picture, or scripture that comes to you. Don't dismiss it, faith believes God speaks and is eager to answer.

Step 5: Obey the Nudge
Ask yourself: "What small act of obedience can I take today in response to what God is showing me?" Write it down and commit to doing it. Faith becomes fiery when it is followed by action.

A Final Faith Builder:
Each time fear whispers in your ear, go back to what God said. Speak it out loud and declare: *"I choose faith over fear. I believe God's word over every lie."*

Here is a prayer to help you build the kind of unshakable, fiery faith that crushes fear and ignites impact:

Dear Lord,

There is truly nothing that you can't do.

The scripture says that Jesus is the founder and finisher of my faith. Well then, Lord please give me the faith that hears your voice with my heart, listens to what you have to say and then ignites me to do what you tell me to do.

You speak to me in so many ways. I don't want to shrug my shoulders and forget what you say to me. I want to be obedient! Through your word, I want to see you as you really are. I want to be who you meant me to be. I want to crush fear and be empowered to live the way you meant me to live.

You love me, and through your love I learn to love myself. I trust you. I want to know you better. I want to be inspired and empowered by you and let your words resonate in my soul. Let the baptism of your Holy Spirit fuel me with faith like fire forever and ever.

In Jesus' name, Amen.

A scripture for you to meditate on:

"Without faith it is impossible to please Him for He that comes to God must believe that He exists and that He is a rewarder of those who diligently seek Him." Hebrews 11:6

Some worship music to help you fuel your faith:

- Amazing Grace *by John Newton*

- Defender *by Stephanie Gretzinger, Springer and Gentile*

- Do It Again *by Brock, Brown, Redman and Furtick.*

- So Will I (100 Billion X)" *by Houston, Hastings and Fatkin*

About Willetta:

Willetta is a faith based singer, speaker, and teacher whose life's mission is to awaken purpose and ignite unshakable faith in women around the world. She is the visionary founder of Fuelled by Faith, a global community devoted to empowering women to build a mountain-moving relationship with God and step into their calling. Willetta is also author of "12 Weeks With Christ!, the first of her Fuelled by Faith Devotional books that empowers women to discover their God given purpose, take bold action and ignite lasting change through faith driven insights and practical steps. If you've ever felt like there's more to your faith journey, more purpose, more power, more intimacy with God, Willetta invites you to join her. It's not too late to become the woman God has called you to be.

Ready to grow your faith and live it out boldly?

For more information about Willetta visit:
www.FueledbyFaith.net

Chapter Six

ANOINTED

For Impact

How to Activate Your Spiritual Gifts to Influence Your Marketplace & Mission.

I never lost my faith in God... I lost faith in myself. My confidence was at rock bottom, and I thought I didn't have the right to speak in church anymore. I falsely believed that I WAS TOO BROKEN TO STAY — so I left, consumed by shame.

How did this all start? I remember sitting in a dingy motel room in downtown Detroit, USA, in 1995. I was alone, scared, and utterly lost. My thoughts raced: "I can't believe they've done this to me! They fired me and dumped me here without the resources to get back to the UK!"

The room was dark, the wallpaper old and flocked. A musty dampness lingered in the air. Outside, the distant hum of traffic on the M1 Michigan Highway, buzzed like static against my ears. But, inside, the silence was deafening. A creeping sensation of dread curled around me. The all-too-familiar dark cloud of depression formed above me, tightening my chest, making each breath feel like a struggle.

My dad had moved to Florida when I was thirteen. He stood about 5'9", with a strong resemblance to Muhammad Ali. We didn't talk as often as I would have liked, but I knew that if I called, he would come. And right now, I needed help.

I picked up the phone, my fingers trembling as I dialled.

"Hello?" His deep, casual voice cut through my panic.

"Dad...hi... it's Vanessa."

"Hey, girl! How ya doing?"

"Dad, I'm in trouble." My voice cracked. Keep it together, Vanessa.

"I got this graduate sales job here in Detroit, but it's not going well. My sales numbers are down, and now they've fired me. They left me in this motel, that looks like something straight out of Psycho!"

I could hear my breathing quickening. The walls of the room seemed to close in as panic set in. But my dad's voice was steady, grounding me in the moment.

"Alright, calm down. I'll fly out and come get you. We'll figure this out."

Relief washed over me, but it was short-lived. The days leading up to my dad's arrival were filled with mounting anxiety. My panic attacks worsened, and my mental state deteriorated rapidly. When my dad arrived, I was barely holding myself together. I had a complete breakdown and required medical attention.

Those weeks in Florida were a blur of tears, exhaustion, and quiet shame. I was grateful to be with family, but deep down, I felt like the biggest failure alive.

The enemy whispered lies:

"You're weak. You're broken. You'll never recover from this."

After a few weeks, I flew back to England and moved in with my mum to heal. When someone breaks a bone or suffers from a visible illness, people instinctively know how to help. But mental illness was different. In the '90s, mental health wasn't something people openly discussed, especially in the church. Fear and misunderstanding kept people at a distance, and I felt like an outcast. I convinced myself that church members would look at me differently, whispering behind my back:

"How can she call herself a Christian if she's so weak-minded?"

This false belief haunted me for years. Rather than face the judgment I imagined, I left the church. I sacrificed my Christian fellowship and connections because I thought it would be easier. I thought I had failed not just myself but my family and my faith.

But here's the thing about God: He never lets His children go.

Even when our faith wavers, even when we allow the enemy to silence us with lies, God's love remains constant.

The Psalmist reminds us of this beautiful truth in Psalm 139:7-10 (NIV):

"Where can I go from your Spirit? Where can I flee from your presence? If I go up to the heavens, you are there; if I make my bed in the depths, you are there. If I rise on the wings of the dawn, if I settle on the far side of the sea, even there your hand will guide me, your right hand will hold me fast."

Just like the shepherd in Jesus' parable who leaves the ninety-nine to find the one lost sheep (Luke 15:3-7), God pursues us in our darkest moments. I was that lost sheep, and yet my Shepherd came searching for me.

This leads me to ask: What is faith?

Faith is stepping up even when you cannot see the whole staircase. GOD wants us to trust Him with the how and not burden ourselves with having all the answers. One scripture that truly resonates with me is:

Proverbs 3:5 (NKJV) "Trust in the Lord with all your heart and lean not on your own understanding."

I had heard this verse many times growing up, but it didn't sink in until I hit rock bottom. I still loved God, but I didn't feel worthy of His love. During my darkest moments of anxiety and self-doubt, I found comfort in Isaiah 41:10 (NIV):

"So do not fear, for I am with you; do not be dismayed, for I am your God. I will strengthen you and help you; I will uphold you with my righteous right hand."

Letting go of my need for control and surrendering to God changed everything. I realized that my worth was never defined by my failures. Who was I to argue with God when He says I am fearfully and wonderfully made? His grace is sufficient, and because of that, I belong in church. I belong in His presence; I have a voice to create impact and so do you.

Once I embraced my worth, I built a life centered around communication, confidence coaching, and speaker training.

I wanted to help women like me uncover their confidence and thrive in all aspects of their lives. I have since guided hundreds of women to find their authentic voice, speak boldly, and lead confidently. They create ripples of impact wherever they go.

That's why I founded The CONFIDENCE CORE, a global movement empowering woman of purpose and faith to live their dreams and create a lasting impact. My own journey from silence to speaking with confidence has become the foundation for helping other women reclaim their voices for the Kingdom.

Reflection Questions:

Where in your life have you felt too broken or unworthy to use your voice?

What lies have you believed about your worth in God's kingdom?

If God were sitting across from you right now, what would He say about those beliefs?

Testimony: Finding Her Voice & Greater Impact

"I always thought I was a confident speaker, but the speaker system showed how to improve our delivery, and I really enjoyed that. I do counselling and, in that environment, usually it's just me and my clients, but there are times when I have to do training and presentations. Today, I'm taking away more confidence in my training and presentation skills thank you."

Pauline Anderson, Shalom Counselling

I want you to live your best life, like Pauline, and show up with confidence, just as I've learned to do through God's grace.

Let's take a moment together now to visualise yourself five years from now. Imagine your best life. Now, write it down in the present tense as if you are already living it.

Be specific:

Action Exercise: Writing Your Vision

- What are you doing?

- Who are you working with?

- Who are you serving?

- How do you feel in this life?

By writing in the present tense, your subconscious will begin to believe it, making you more likely to take the necessary steps to bring it to life.

Journaling Prompts:

What specific limiting beliefs are holding you back from speaking your truth?

Write down what you believe God would say about these limiting beliefs.

What is one small step you can take this week to begin using your voice again?

Always remember this... You are not too broken, too late, or too unqualified to make an impact. God has anointed you for such a time as this, and every scar, setback, and season of silence has prepared you to rise in boldness. Your voice carries the authority of Heaven, your gifts are designed to shift people, and your story will set others free.

Walk forward knowing that you are chosen, equipped, and unstoppable in Him. The world is waiting for the impact that only you can make.

I wish you joy and success on this journey.

With love, Vanessa.

Here is a prayer to help you activate your spiritual gifts to influence your marketplace & mission:

Dear Lord,

I pray that my vision is clear, compelling, and filled with divine momentum. Guide me through my challenges, strengthening my faith with each obstacle I overcome. Let my struggles become lessons that shape me into a wiser, stronger vessel for Your purpose.

Celebrate with me in my victories, and let my light shine brightly, inspiring those around me. Help me to walk in confidence, knowing that I am worthy, loved, and called for something greater.

In Jesus' name, Amen.

A scripture for you to meditate on:

"For God has not given us a spirit of fear, but of power and of love and of a sound mind." 2 Timothy 1:7

Some worship songs to help you dream with God

- Thy Word by *Amy Grant*

- Break Every Chain *by Jesus Culture*

- God Will Work it Out *feat. Israel Houghton & Mav City Gospel Choir*

- I Know Who I Am *by Sinach*

About Vanessa:

Vanessa is a multi-award-winning international speaker, author, and certified confidence and speaker coach with over two decades of expertise in corporate communication. Passionate about helping women find their voice, she has empowered hundreds to speak boldly and lead confidently. As the founder of the Global Confidence Core Movement for mainly faith-based professional women, Vanessa is on a mission to break barriers and ignite self-belief. Through her signature programme The Transformative Life Launchpad Programme™ and her Pearl Speaking Pathway™ speaker programme, she equips women with practical tools to thrive in leadership, business, and life.

Vanessa's clients have gone on to speak confidently on stages and show up with more impact in their personal and professional lives. Are you ready to step into your God-given power and purpose? Connect with Vanessa today:

Visit
https://linktr.ee/vanessafraterrobertson

Chapter Seven

HOLY SPIRIT

Strategy

How to operate in divine wisdom, prophetic clarity, and live a supernatural life.

"Why are you going back to Barcelona? You know you're meant to be in Texas. Why are you putting Barcelona in the way?"

The strong male voice in my right ear made me jump out of my skin. Just moments before, I'd been quietly mesmerized by the midnight moon glistening across the water where our boat was moored. It was November 23rd, 2023, and my mind was on the beautiful apartment in Barcelona we were moving into a few days later, while mentally ticking off my checklist during the last dog walk of the night.

Nobody was ever around at that time, so who could it be? I spun around, heart racing, expecting a giant man to match the giant voice... nothing. Still reeling, I climbed down the hatch stairs and found Greg in the kitchen.

"I need to tell you something," he said with a serious look on his face. "I've had another word."

I leaned in. "Okay, what did He say this time?"

"Don't go back to Barcelona. Texas is your spiritual homeland. Go now." I laughed in disbelief. Greg frowned. "It isn't that funny."

"I'm not laughing at you," I said. "I just had the same word while I was out walking the dogs. What should we do?"

He didn't hesitate. "We go."

Follow the Breadcrumbs...

To understand the weight of that moment, you need to know this: four months earlier, Greg had received his very first word from God. We'd flown to Texas in July 2023 to help a client with her podcast before speaking at a Vegas conference. As she picked us up from the airport, she announced in her strong Texan accent: "Just so y'all know, we're not gonna be working on my podcast while you're here. God told me last night that you're about to go to your next level of leadership with Him and I'm to prepare you for that."

We were stunned. I wasn't a Christian. Greg was a card-carrying Humanist; adamant God didn't exist. On paper, we were the least likely candidates for His mission. And yet, God had a plan. Step-by-step, He was leading us. All we had to do was follow the breadcrumbs.

As she poured into me, Holy Spirit was quietly working on Greg too. Without him even realizing, God's love was massaging its way into his spirit. Over the next few days, our friend shared the Father's heart, taught us how to hear Holy Spirit, how to speak our spirit language, and stirred a burning faith unlike anything we'd known before.

On our final day in Texas, just four hours before leaving for Vegas, Greg and I were relaxing when he suddenly turned to me.

"I've had a word from God."

I laughed. "Oh ha-ha, very funny. Stop mucking about. You don't even believe in God."

"I know," he said, his face deadpan. "I'm serious. God spoke to me." My jaw dropped. This was the man who had sworn God didn't exist! "What did He say?"

"Texas is your spiritual homeland. You need to be here."

I stared at him, stunned. "Wait, what? Homeland. Why would He say that? And why would He say it to you? You don't even believe in God!"
"I know! Seriously Sammy, I'm more surprised than you are."

"How can you be sure this word is from God?" I pressed.

"I just know it is."

Greg wasn't joking, I knew that much. My mind was spinning. "Well, can you tell God it's very inconvenient right now. We've already started the immigration process for Barcelona. Texas will have to wait!"

If you've ever tried to negotiate with God, you'll know that what He starts, He finishes (Philippians 1:6). We chuckled, but the weight of it lingered. Within hours we were on a flight to Vegas, unsure what to do with this newfound connection to our Creator, yet aware something significant had already shifted.

On our way home, we stopped back in Texas. After long talks with our friend, every question answered and every doubt met, we gave our lives to Christ and were baptized in her pool on July 31, 2023, the day before flying back to the UK.

We returned to our travels and even found an apartment in Barcelona, but something deep inside had changed. Later we'd learn the truth of Proverbs 16:1:

"The plans of the heart belong to man, but the answer of the tongue is from the Lord."

If You Want to Make God Laugh, Tell Him YOUR plans!

We were about to sign the apartment paperwork in Barcelona when Greg was called back to the UK for a funeral. We both felt a nudge not to sign it before we left. At the time, we called it "intuition" or "gut instinct." Now we know it was Holy Spirit guiding us.

We also felt prompted to pack everything into the car and drive back, even though we could have left it there. After all, we'd be back in a week, right? But the Lord had other plans.

As Greg had said, "We go," the breadcrumb trail of God's plan became clearer. All the time we were going through the Spanish immigration process, God was preparing us for the American immigration paperwork. "His thoughts are higher than our thoughts, and His ways higher than our ways" (Isaiah 55:8-9).

Within two days, I was on a plane to Dallas. Less than a week later, I'd signed a rental contract on a home near the lake and engaged immigration lawyers. We moved boldly, trusting God to make our paths straight... and He did.

Greg picked me up from Heathrow airport on December 3rd, 2023, ready to pack up our life in the UK. With our Texas contract starting January 1st, we had just 33 days to give everything away and go. As we prayed about what to take, Holy Spirit highlighted Genesis 19:26: "But Lot's wife, behind him, looked back, and she became a pillar of salt."

"Ok, there's our confirmation," we said. "There's no looking back now!" We decided only to tell our inner work circle at first, while we took time to understand what this all meant. People already thought we were crazy moving to Texas instead of Barcelona, so what would they think if they knew we were really giving up all our worldly belongings, income, home, everything we'd ever built and everything we'd ever known to follow the call of God on our lives? We weren't ready for that potential debate yet, so we kept it in our own hearts to start with.

Christianity 101...

When I picked up my first Bible, I thought Christians knew every scripture by heart, like some kind of "Christianity 101" test! I pressured myself for months, trying to memorize verses in case I got quizzed. But the deeper God's word breathed into me, the less I cared what people thought and I started to marinate in the scriptures instead.

I began reading the Bible like a love letter to all His children (yes, it's His love letter to you and I too), soaking it in one verse at a time. I spent hours every morning falling in love with His word, growing in relationship with Him, and discovering His personality. I studied deeply, realizing God was nothing like the wrathful, condemning, religious figure I'd heard about. He was pursuing my heart, just like He's pursuing yours, so the more I got to know His voice and tone, the easier it became to recognize the fruits of His Spirit (Galatians 5:22–23), versus the enemy's lies.

Finding Your Purpose Isn't Always Elegant...
Sometimes You Crash into It!

Since starting ministry, we've met so many believers weighed down with guilt or shame, thinking life should get easier once they follow Jesus. When things get tough though, they assume one or more of the following ten things:

I'm a bad believer.

God is punishing me.

I must have sinned and opened a door I shouldn't have.

God isn't answering my prayers, so He clearly doesn't love me.

If I had more faith, this wouldn't be happening.

God is disappointed in me.

Other Christians seem to have it all together, so what's wrong with me?

I need to fix myself before coming to God.

My past disqualifies me from being used by God.

If God loves me, I shouldn't be struggling.

Sis, these thoughts aren't Biblical. They're the enemy's whispers, designed to make you question your identity. If Satan can do that, he can sink your ship before you even notice the leak. But Jesus came so you could have life to the full (John 10:10).

Yes, from earth's view, things may look like they're falling apart, but from Heaven's view, God is setting you up for harvest... As long as you stay close to the vine (John 15:5). Look at Job. After everything he went through, God blessed him with twice as much (Job 42:10).

We learned to trust God the hard way. Four months after arriving in Texas, a woman crashed into our car, writing it off. Our first thought was: *"What did we do wrong?"* But it wasn't the enemy. It was God's creative way of providing.

Miracle One:
The insurance company paid out abundantly within 48 hours and gave us a $900 rental car for two weeks free of charge.

Miracle Two:
When we found a new car, a friend, following God's instruction, bought it for us and said God told them to reward us for our obedience. Not only did we drive away in our beautiful new car, but the insurance money was enough to cover our rent for the next eight months.

And just when we thought those were the blessings...
the real ones were still to come!

Ongoing Miracles...

I'd bought Greg surprise tickets to see The Chosen season 4 on Easter weekend, and it happened to start the very night of the crash. With no rental car until the following morning, we had no choice but to grab a taxi. That's how we met Tommy.

On the ride home, we got chatting. After sharing some of his story and hearing a bit of ours, he asked, "Which church do you go to?"

"We don't go to church," we said.

Tommy's head whipped around so fast I worried he'd swerve off the freeway. "What do you mean you don't go to church? Everyone living in the Bible Belt goes to church!"

Without missing a beat, he asked if we wanted to go on Sunday. Greg and I exchanged a glance. "Yes," we heard ourselves say. By the time we pulled into our driveway, this once ordinary taxi ride had turned into a divine appointment. Tommy prayed for us right there in the car, then texted to confirm he'd pick us up Sunday at noon for the afternoon service.

Two days later, we stepped foot in a church together for the first time and it felt like coming home. Gateway Frisco quickly became more than a church. It became our family. They discipled us, equipped us, and gave us the firm foundation we needed to step into ministry confidently. Tommy became a dear friend, as did so many others over those next eleven months.

What looked like a curse (the crash), turned out to be the very moment God steered us into destiny. We drove away with more than a new car and eight months of rent paid. We drove into the very ministry we were born for. It turns out we had to crash into our purpose to find it.

You're Going to Bring 100,000 People Back to Faith...

Six months later, after pouring ourselves into serving at Gateway, I woke up one January morning with a strong deposit in my spirit. Over and over, it came: You're going to bring 100,000 people back to faith.

Half asleep, I croaked, "You must be crazy, Lord. How can we bring 100,000 people back to faith? We've only been Christians five minutes. Who's going to listen to us?"

But He wouldn't relent. At 5am, I gave up trying to sleep and spent the day praying and journaling. One word kept surfacing... lights. But I still wasn't getting it.

That evening, as I uploaded our next Empowering Prayers podcast, a vision appeared. A globe, about six inches in height hovered just four inches away from my face, turning slowly. Thin beams of light began popping up all over it, like glowing toothpicks lighting up the room.

"See all these pillars of light, Sammy?" Holy Spirit said. Then two hands appeared, cupping the globe from below, gently gathering the lights upward.

"These are women all over the world who are currently working alone to bring Heaven to earth. Look how much stronger they'll be when you bring these lights together."

The beams fused into one blazing pillar that was so bright I squinted to look.

"Your purpose this season, Sammy, is to bring the lights together. Your role is to equip them. Your assignment is to start with a book."

I was curious. "Oh Lord, this is so big. Where do you want me to start?" "Get a pen," He said.

For the next three hours He poured out the vision for the Kingdom Catalysts ministry, Kingdom Women community, Kingdom Women events, retreats, and the very book you're holding now in your hands.

Stepping Into Obedience...

After that, I began waking daily with dreams of women I hadn't spoken to in years. Some had been Christians all their lives. Others had come to Christ since we last spoke. One wasn't yet a believer but was feeling drawn to church. God had already gone ahead like a pillar of fire, preparing their hearts for my call.

Still, I procrastinated. "They'll think I'm crazy when I say God told me to contact them," I argued with Him. But when I finally obeyed, each one instantly knew it was a divine assignment.

If I've learned anything, it's this: God always gets His way. His will, will be done. He's already in your future. He sees what you can't yet see. When He calls you, just say yes and amen, then trust Him to equip you step-by-step. What He calls you to, He'll call you through... but in His timing, not yours.

A New Assignment...

In February 2025, Greg and I returned to the UK for two business events and our first Kingdom Women Catalysts retreat. From the moment we landed, we felt a strange sense we were supposed to move back. We tried to ignore it, until Greg's back went into excruciating pain, landing him in hospital with two slipped discs. He couldn't travel and needed an MRI with at least two weeks of recovery in England.

Then, the morning I was due to fly back to Texas alone, God woke me at 5am. "Sammy, be prepared. You are coming back to the UK."

I resisted with every excuse... our impending book launch that was meant to be that same month, our life and ministry work in Texas. But He showed me vision after vision, like a movie reel, of people we'd touched during that week in the UK. The evidence was undeniable. His Spirit had moved powerfully through us here.

Even when I returned to Texas, the signs kept piling up. My flight was a nightmare when I was almost denied boarding due to their error with my ticket. Then I was pulled aside for interrogation when I landed in America and threatened with deportation because of new US immigration laws that had been enforced while I was in the UK. I had all the paperwork to show and everything was okay, but by the time I got home, I was shaken and exhausted.

That's when God spoke again: "You were never meant to be here this long, Sammy. You're ready. You're going back, so get ready to move."

Half-asleep and very cranky, I muttered, "But God, I just bought that lovely big scripture for my office wall. Where am I going to put it if not here?"

"I'm sorry, Sammy," He replied tenderly. "You're not going to have a wall to put that on for a while. Start packing."

Back to the UK...

By March 3rd, our flights were booked for March 30th. Less than a month to give everything away... *again.*

As we prayed together over Zoom, God revealed visions of us traveling full-time across the UK. "Looks like it's time to renovate a van or bus like we dreamed of doing a few years ago," Greg joked.

Two weeks later, Greg was fit enough to fly out and help me with the packing and a few weeks after that, our Gateway family loaded us, our luggage, and three dogs into their cars, driving us to Dallas Fort Worth airport. Our spiritual mom, Su Park (chapter 2 of this book), prayed and prophesied over us: "When you land in London, you'll be given your first assignment."

She was right.

Within an hour of landing, while sipping coffee in the arrivals lounge at Heathrow airport, a South African family struck up conversation. Out of nowhere, our new friend Dave from Cape Town, pointed at us and said, "You need to go and see Damien Carr at Hope Church in Corby."

Just like that... we got our first UK assignment!

On the way to Corby, we spotted a lovely 17-seater minibus for sale, panoramic windows and all. "That would make a perfect conversion," we said. Two days later, we'd bought it, boarded our cases and dogs, and then stopped at the store for a camping stove, air mattress, and portable loo.

When we finally arrived at Hope Church, we discovered it was part of the Elim network - an organization with over 500 church plants across the UK and Europe since 1915. We stood in awe. God hadn't just sent us to a home church. He'd sent us to a network of churches already marked out for the journey He planned for us. His detail, His timing, His orchestration, it was flawless.

God is good... ALL the time!

After two years of experiencing the unrelenting grace, vision, and generosity of our Almighty Creator, I could fill ten more books with stories of what He's done (don't worry, we will!) And please make sure to join us at one of our next 'She is Awakened' events or retreats to continue your journey with us beyond this book! But for now, I want to leave you with some Holy Spirit lessons that you can immediately apply in your life. Let's go!

Step 1. Obedience Unlocks Strategy...

"**Revelation** when met with **obedience** leads to **confirmation** and then the **blessing** flows." Our dear friend, Dr Tom Taylor, impressed this truth on us repeatedly: "When God says GO don't wait for more confirmation. Just do what He said!"

Revelation Activity:
Sit quietly with God. Remove distractions and thank Him for all He is doing in and through your life. Say, 'Lord, have your way in me' and ask Him to show you what He wants you to know, see, or do next. Lift up prayers of gratitude for the vision coming your way and write down everything that comes into your mind, ideally in your journal if you have one.

Step 2. Trust Him...

Faith means moving even when the next step isn't fully clear. Waiting for more confirmation shows distrust. What many call intuition or gut instinct is really Holy Spirit prompting you toward God's purposes. Ignoring it is ignoring His hand in your life.

Obedience Activity:
Look at what you wrote in Step 1, then list the actions you could take immediately. Hover over each one in prayer, asking Holy Spirit for a "yes" or "no." If unsure, pick one and start. Closed doors are just guidance to move to the next opportunity until you find the open one.

Step 3. Back it Up with Scripture...

Every word, feeling, or nudge from Holy Spirit should be confirmed with scripture. Sit quietly, place your hand over your Bible, and ask Him to guide you. Let your fingers rest on the pages until a passage draws your attention. Read it slowly, several times if needed, and write down the insights.
Over time, patterns emerge, helping you distinguish God's voice from your own thoughts or the enemy's deception.

Confirmation Activity:
Apply this process to your revelations and record the outcomes.
Over time, you'll quickly see how God speaks specifically to you in all the areas of your life.

Step 4. It Rarely Makes Sense...

God's breadcrumbs often seem confusing at first. Follow them anyway, step-by-step. Obedience brings you to where He is already working. The reality that always blows my mind is that He doesn't need us, but He wants us to partner with Him anyway! So, step into His plans, and you'll find yourself daily in the centre of His will, where blessings flow naturally, like rivers of living water.

Blessing Activity:
Journal all the blessings you've received in the past month. Thank God for each one. The more you notice His fingerprints, the more you'll see them daily, because He is able to do far more abundantly than all you ask or think (Ephesians 3:20).

Sis, we're at the end of our time together for now and I'm so excited for you!

I encourage you wholeheartedly to apply these four steps consistently, and your life will overflow with blessings and miracles. You are more ready than you have any way of knowing, so step out in radical faith and be an unstoppable Catalyst for the Kingdom.

Remember, you are fearfully and wonderfully made (Psalm 139:14), and this is your time to shine!

Lots of love
Sammy xxx

Some scriptures for you to meditate on as you step into Holy Spirit's Strategy for your life:

"His thoughts are higher than our thoughts, and His ways higher than our ways." Isaiah 55:8–9 NKJV

"But the fruit of the Spirit is love, joy, peace, patience, kindness, goodness, faithfulness, gentleness and self-control. Against such things there is no law." Galatians 5:22–23 NIV

"Ask, and it will be given to you; search, and you will find; knock, and the door will be opened for you. For everyone who asks receives, and everyone who searches finds, and for everyone who knocks, the door will be opened." Matthew 7:7-8

A prayer to help you operate in divine wisdom, prophetic clarity, and live a supernatural life:

Heavenly Father,

Thank You for Your love and for the plans You have for me. Today, I receive Your divine wisdom to guide my thoughts, decisions, and steps (James 1:5).

Holy Spirit, open my ears to hear Your voice, my eyes to see Your guidance, and my heart to respond with faith and obedience.

Lord, remove every doubt, fear, and distraction, and help me trust You in every moment. Align my life and ministry with Your purposes so that I may walk boldly, speak prophetically, and live a supernatural life (John 10:10). Let every word I speak and every action I take flow with Your favor and power.

I declare that I am equipped, empowered, and unstoppable, a vessel of Your wisdom, a carrier of Your light, and a partner in bringing Heaven to earth.

May Your Kingdom work through me today and always.

In Jesus' name, Amen.

Some worship music to help you welcome Holy Spirit in:

- Holy Spirit You are Welcome Here *by Jesus Culture, Kim Walker Smith*

- House of Miracles *by DOE Essential Worship*

- Centre *by Bethel Music, Abbie Gamboa*

- That's Who I Praise *by Brandon Lake*

About Sammy:

With over 1000 business growth resources published online, 10 best-selling books authored, and multiple international awards earned, Sammy Garrity is a voice of inspiration to Christian women internationally.

As co-founder of The Impact Catalysts and Director of Evangelism for The Kingdom Catalysts Ministry, Sammy turned her attention to equipping Christian women to fulfil their God-given purpose and eternal impact when she and husband Greg gave their lives to Christ in July 2023.

Having mentored over 71,000 mission driven leaders to build successful businesses since 2002, surveying over 41,000 of them about what stops them succeeding, God is now using Sammy's experience and resources for the Kingdom, teaching and equipping women to boldly step into their God-given calling.

For more information about Sammy and the programs they deliver at Kingdom Catalysts, Visit:
www.ChristianBusinessResources.com

Connect with Sammy in the Kingdom Women Facebook Group at:
www.facebook.com/groups/kingdomwomencatalysts

Chapter Eight

COURAGE

Over Comfort

How to leave behind the safety of silence to roar with Heaven's boldness.

"The Lord is my shepherd; I shall not want. He makes me lie down in green pastures; He leads me beside quiet waters.
He restores my soul…" (Psalm 23)

That Psalm has been an anchor for me. It reminds me that no matter what I face, God has been with me, guiding me, comforting me, and whispering courage into places where silence has tried to limit me.

Looking back, I wish I'd had that Psalm during my tumultuous childhood. My parents split up when I was five, and after that my mother, my brother, and I moved around a lot. We were often short of money, and my mom was searching for stability in her own way, looking for love, as the song says, in all the wrong places. She did her best, but for us as children, it meant being dropped into new situations repeatedly.

I was often the outsider in the school playground, trying to make friends quickly. Soon after, we would pack up from wherever we lived and move on again. One memory stands out very clearly: we had just moved to a new town, and my uncle gave my mom a car to help her start afresh. The three of us (my brother, mum and I) shared a room with stretcher beds, using a cardboard box as a table. We ate porridge three times a day while Mom worked to provide for us.

I came from a very clever and educated family, but both of my parents were working through their own struggles. It felt like some of the challenges they faced were inherited, and I, in turn, carried some of that weight too. I didn't always know how to manage it, so I often just stood on my own, trying to muster courage in each new situation.

Faith would later become the thing that helped me find that courage, though at the time I didn't know much about God. My parents weren't church-going or practicing Christians, simply good people doing their best.

When I was still quite young, my mom had to go in for an operation. With my dad living in another town, she had nobody to care for us, so my brother and I were sent to stay at a Catholic orphanage for three months. I still remember one of the nuns giving me a skipping rope. My brother stayed in a dorm with all the younger kids, while I was placed with the nuns.

Because it was a Catholic orphanage, we attended services three times a day. We recited catechisms, joined in the prayers, and followed the rhythm of convent life. For a child, it was both strange and fascinating. I didn't realize it then, but those months planted something in me, a sense of awe, a sense that there was something bigger than me.

After three months, we returned home to Mom, and life went on. But by the time I was thirteen, I was sent to boarding school. That school gave me a sense of stability between the ages of thirteen and seventeen. We attended church every Sunday, and our uniforms - black with white collars and cuffs in the winter, white in the summer, made us look a little like nuns as we marched together to the service.

Boarding school was strict, often lonely, but it taught me about community, kindness, and the importance of having an inner light. It was in those years that I started to believe there really was something greater guiding me, even if I didn't yet have words for it. That thought, that light, kept me going. A few years later, I was confirmed in the church, and faith began to play a more active role in my life.

As I grew older and entered the corporate world, I carried those early lessons with me, but they were tested in ways I couldn't have anticipated. The environments I worked in were high-pressure and often male-dominated. I found myself silenced, not because I didn't have ideas, but because I doubted whether my voice was worth hearing.

When I first started working in these companies, I began to slowly find my voice. I started to speak up when I didn't agree with things, when I could see there was a better way, or when decisions simply didn't feel right. And, of course, that got me into trouble. People don't always like the truth. And that's really what this chapter is about, learning how to choose courage over comfort.

What I had to understand quickly is that not everyone is at the same place in life. Not everyone has had the same experiences. Not everyone is self-aware or reflective of how their actions impact others. If you want to lead with courage, you need to meet people where they are, not where you think they should be. You must adjust your behaviour and your feedback so that people can understand, connect, and come along with you on the journey. It takes patience and time.

When I first stepped into leadership, I was taught to be authoritarian, "tell people what to do, make the decisions, enforce the rules." But I soon realized that doesn't work. People don't follow unless they feel empowered. Leadership isn't about standing in an ivory tower; it's about guiding, enabling, and respecting those around you.

One of the defining experiences for me was my early work in South Africa, right after Nelson Mandela's release from prison. I remember hearing on the news about this "terrorist" who was going to be freed, and thinking, 'Oh my gosh, this is terrifying'. Then my boss called me in and said, "You're in charge of the empowerment and diversity programs. You need to bring people together, different races, different cultures. You need to create understanding, dialogue, even reconciliation."

And so, I ran those programs. I witnessed moments that changed me forever. People would speak up about the injustices they had faced, and sometimes they broke down and cried in front of everyone. I could see the raw empathy that came when we simply listened to one another's stories. I realized just how often we judge because we don't understand, because we haven't walked in someone else's shoes, because we feel superior without even knowing it.

And yet, even in those moments, I didn't always speak up as boldly as I could have. I remember an Indian boss who wasn't allowed to sit on the board of directors because of his heritage. I felt it was wrong, but at the time, I stayed silent. If I were in that position now, I know I would have said something. I've learned that courage is not about being reckless, it's about speaking out from the right place, guided by principle, empathy, and integrity.

One of the hardest lessons came toward the end of my corporate career. I was told to dismiss a senior leader, a man who simply didn't fit in with the leadership team. He had done nothing wrong. I had to take his lanyard, clear his desk, and walk him out. He was crying, explaining that his wife was ill, and I just followed along. I felt deep empathy, but I didn't speak out. I stayed in line with the pack.

It's a moment I will never forget. And it taught me a critical lesson: empathy alone is not enough. If you see injustice, if you know something isn't right, you must act. You must speak out. Sitting on the fence, staying silent for the sake of comfort, doesn't protect anyone, it only allows the wrong to continue.

That was when I truly understood that courage isn't optional. It's a responsibility. Speaking up isn't about you taking center stage and being in the limelight; it's about being true to yourself and standing for what's right, even when it's hard.

The enemy is subtle like that. He whispers lies: "Stay safe. Don't risk it. What if they laugh? What if you fail?" But God's Spirit kept stirring in me, reminding me that courage is not the absence of fear, it's choosing to speak and act in obedience despite fear.

Over time, I began to learn that courage over comfort means partnering with Heaven's boldness. It means opening my mouth when God gives me words to say. It means trusting that obedience releases miracles, not just for me, but for those around me.

I've had to unlearn the lies of my past: that I was too broken, too ordinary, or too unworthy to have influence. And I now embrace the truth that I am made in the image of a courageous God, filled with His Spirit, anointed for impact.

Activity: The Life Timeline

One practice that has helped me step out of silence and into boldness is something I call the Life Timeline. It's simple but powerful:

Draw a line across a page
On the left, write "Childhood," and on the right, write "Today."

Mark key moments
Place dots along the line for the moments that shaped you, both painful and joyful. Write a word or short phrase to describe each one.

Look for God's hand
Ask: Where was God at work, even when I didn't see Him? What did I learn? What courage did I gain?

Spot the patterns
Notice how challenges built your resilience, how times of silence shaped listening, how steps of faith led to breakthroughs.

Claim your boldness
Circle one moment where you stayed silent but wish you hadn't. Now write: Next time, I will choose courage over comfort.

This activity will help you see your story from Heaven's perspective. It reminds you that every moment, good or bad, has equipped you for boldness today.

A Final Word of Encouragement

Friend, you were never meant to hide in the shadows or silence your voice. You were made in the image of a bold, courageous God.
His Spirit lives in you, and He has already anointed you for impact.
So, step forward with expectancy. Speak boldly when He nudges.
Act when He prompts. It's not comfort that will release Heaven on Earth, it's your courage that will do that, not just for you, but for those who are waiting for your voice.

With love,
Desiree.

A scripture for you to meditate on as you choose courage over comfort:

"The LORD is my shepherd, I lack nothing. He makes me lie down in green pastures, he leads me beside quiet waters, he refreshes my soul. He guides me along the right paths for his name's sake. Even though I walk through the darkest valley, I will fear no evil, for you are with me; your rod and your staff, they comfort me. You prepare a table before me in the presence of my enemies. You anoint my head with oil, my cup overflows. Surely your goodness and love will follow me all the days of my life, and I will dwell in the house of the LORD forever."
Psalm 23 NIV

A prayer to help you leave behind the safety of silence and roar with Heaven's boldness:

God, thank You for never leaving me, even in the times I felt most lost or afraid.

Thank You for planting seeds of faith in me from childhood, and for showing me that my voice matters in Your Kingdom. I ask for fresh courage today that I will choose obedience over fear, boldness over silence and courage over comfort.

Fill me with Heaven's boldness to roar with Your truth and release miracles wherever I go.

In your Holy name I pray, Amen.

Some worship music to help you step into courage:

- Lord Make me an Instrument of your peace by *Sr Breige O'Hare*

- Morning Has Broken by *Eleanor Farjeon*

- Jerusalem Jerusalem (words by William Blake), music by *Sir Hubert Parry*

- Holy! Holy! Holy! Lord God Almighty! by *Reginald Heber*

About Desiree:

Desiree Parsons (nee Anderson) is a multiple bestselling author and writer. She has a background in corporate HR, Training and Development with leading companies. She is a master level coach, keynote speaker and is a passionate mental health first aider.

She encourages heart-led entrepreneurs to live a life of integrity and rise to claim their full potential in life and work.

For more information and to connect with Desiree visit:

LinkedIn
www.linkedin.com/in/desiree-a-crestcoachingandhr

Chapter Nine

BIRTHING

Kingdom

Ideas

How to steward and birth God-given ideas as a catalyst of change.

As I sit at my black glass desk in my turquoise-and-white garden office, sunlight spilling through the window, I often whisper to myself: "How did I get here?" The trophies, the books, the photos on the shelves behind me tell one story – of success, impact, and legacy. But another memory plays across my mind like a cinema reel: the bailiff at my old front door, ready to strip away what little my two children and I had left at the time. How did I get from there... to this? The only answer: God, grit, and unrelenting belief.

One of my favourite songs comes to mind by Travis Greene, "You Made a Way."

You see, back in 2004, my reality was far from this office. I was a young mother locked in a cycle of domestic abuse – mental, verbal, and physical. The many nights crouched in my bedroom, heart racing, praying my children didn't hear the violence that erupted within those four walls. I carried the weight of a tumour diagnosis, the fear of paralysis, and the shame of silence. My journals became my escape, though my friend Nicky would constantly warn me: "Michelle, you can't just write it all away; one day it could be your eulogy we're writing, instead of you writing inside a journal."

The awful truth is – she was right.

Eventually, I summoned the courage to leave the marriage. But walking out the door didn't mean walking into healing. That part was slow, messy, and often unbearable. There were nights I cried myself to sleep, mornings I wished I hadn't woken up, and dark moments when I tried to end it all – yes, I almost killed this girl.

Freedom didn't silence the torment. I was stalked. My house was broken into. My clothes were torn and destroyed; symbols of my life ripped apart piece by piece.

The truth is these lines can't contain the whole story. What I endured was more than broken things; it was the breaking of me. He didn't just unravel my sanity; he stripped away my identity. I no longer recognized the

woman in the mirror. Leaving was only the first step.
Rebuilding meant learning, slowly, painfully, that my worth wasn't lost in what he tried to destroy. Slowly, I began to piece myself back together, through counselling, my faith, personal growth, and through the quiet power of writing.

At first it was just journaling, spilling my thoughts onto the page to make sense of the chaos. Then came the whisper of something more: the courage to try writing my first book. But with every sentence, doubt pressed down like a heavy hand. The lies I had carried for years still haunted me - you're not good enough, no one will ever read this, who do you think you are?

That's when I realized the truth that cut deep: even though he was no longer in my life, I was still giving him power. I was letting his voice control my state of mind, chaining me to a dungeon of unforgiveness and bitterness. I had opened the door as well to the enemy to lie to me about my identity - a bit like the serpent deceiving Eve in the Garden of Eden.

By the grace and mercy of God I pushed through doubt, fear, and the lies that had tried to silence me - and I wrote my first book (Overcome & Rise Above - How To Turn The Downside of Your Challenges Into The Upside Of Renewing Your Life). To my amazement, it became a bestseller! That one act of courage unlocked doors I never imagined: speaking invitations poured in, and mentorship opportunities allowed me to transform my pain into a platform. What the enemy had meant to destroy me; God used as fuel to shape my calling.

Before long, I was standing in places I once thought were unreachable. One of the most humbling moments was receiving a commendation from the late Her Majesty Queen Elizabeth for my work in the community, supporting women and parents raising children with special needs. That part of the journey was born out of my own experience of parenting my son who had special needs - but that's a story for another time.

Today, I am Michelle Watson - bestselling author, having written five books and co-authored four multi-award-winning books, international speaker, mentor, deacon, wife, a proud mother of three and owner of a seven-figure business. But titles aren't the real testimony.

The true story is this: God can take broken pieces and craft them into a Kingdom masterpiece.

You see I used to ask the famous question that so many do, and maybe even you have. 'Why me?'

There were times when I questioned God, 'Why this? Why me?'
But Romans 8:28 reminded me: even the broken pieces are part of the masterpiece. My trials weren't wasted; they became the training ground for my calling.

"And we know that in all things God works for the good of those who love him, who have been called according to his purpose."
Romans 8:28.

If there is one scripture that has been the steady anchor in the storms and sunshine of my life, that is it. Those words have been more than ink on a page to me; they have been oxygen when I couldn't breathe, a compass when I lost direction, and a promise when I felt forgotten. I never imagined that my story, marked by pain, setbacks, and impossible odds, would become a testimony that could empower others. The fire of domestic abuse, the crushing weight of depression, the suffocating grip of financial hardship, and the dark valley of despair that whispered I should end it all was all only a tip of the iceberg of the many challenges I was still yet to face. And yet, through every valley and every battle, I've witnessed how God weaves pain into purpose.

Today, I stand not just as a survivor, but as a thriver. My scars have become my testimony, and my life's work is to help others do the same – to turn their pain into platforms, their purpose into profit, and their stories into books and onto stages. What once tried to silence me has become the very thing God uses to amplify my voice for others. Romans 8:28 is the thread that runs through every part of my story. When I look back now, I see not random struggles, but divine strategy that has helped not just me, but every life He allows me to touch.

So, I write these words as both a witness and a warrior:
Whatever you are walking through, hold on. ALL THINGS, not SOME, not a FEW, but ALL things – are working together for your good.

I have learned that God often hides His greatest treasures in our darkest seasons. Looking back, the ideas, visions, and strategies He placed in me were not random sparks of creativity, they were Kingdom ideas, divine seeds planted in soil that looked barren. When I stewarded those Kingdom ideas, they became catalysts of change. From the pain of abuse came my passion to give women a voice. From financial lack was birthed a vision to teach others how to turn purpose into profit. From depression arose the mission to help people rediscover hope and balance. Each trial was really a womb of transformation, and my responsibility was not to abort the process but to carry it through to delivery and now I have also become a 'Mid-wife' for others.

Birthing Kingdom ideas requires stewardship: protecting the seed, nurturing it through prayer, refining it through faith, and pushing even when it feels uncomfortable. It means trusting that even in seasons of waiting, God is aligning everything for His glory and our good.

Today, the initiatives, books, and platforms I've built are living testimonies that when you birth what God places inside of you, it doesn't just change your life - it changes generations.

So, if you are carrying a God-given idea right now, don't dismiss it, don't delay it, and don't despise the process. Steward it well. Protect it, nurture it, and prepare for delivery. Because Romans 8:28 reminds us that every setback, every struggle, and every stage of the journey is part of the divine plan.

Practical Stewardship Keys for Birthing Kingdom Ideas:

Pray It Through
Cover your idea in prayer daily. Ask God for clarity, timing, and wisdom to steward it well.

Write It Down
Document the vision. A seed becomes clearer when it's taken out of your head and placed on paper (Habakkuk 2:2).

Seek Wise Counsel
Share your idea with trusted mentors or faith-filled leaders who can advise, affirm, and challenge you.

Prepare in Faith
Take small, consistent steps. Invest in learning, resources, and disciplines that align with the vision.

Push in the Process
Don't give up when it feels uncomfortable or delayed. Birth requires labour, stay the course and trust the promise.

A Prayer to Birth Kingdom Ideas:

Father, thank You for turning my pain into purpose and my scars into a testimony of Your goodness. I give You every broken chapter and every healed one, knowing You waste nothing. Lord, stir up the kingdom ideas in me that You've planted. Give me courage to push through fear, strength to endure the stretching, and faith to believe that what You've conceived in me will come to life. May I rise from the ashes of my past, confident that no wound disqualifies me from Your plan. Knowing that all things work together for my good, to build Your Kingdom and impact generations.

In Jesus' Name, Amen.

Some worship music to help fuel your Kingdom ideas:

- Promises *(feat. Joe L Barnes & Naomi Raine) by Maverick City | TRIBL*
- Fear is Not My Future *by Elevation & Maverick City Music*
- Firm Foundation *by Maverick City Music*
- Can't Give Up Now *by Mary Mary*

About Michelle:

Michelle Watson is a multi-award-winning international speaker, bestselling author, business and book mentor, and podcast host with a mission to empower individuals worldwide. A survivor of domestic abuse, depression, and suicidal tendencies, she inspires others through her powerful storytelling skills and her vulnerability in sharing her experiences on numerous large platforms. Michelle helps entrepreneurs and businesses amplify their visibility, influence, and vision, creating impactful stories and lasting legacies worldwide.

She specialises in guiding clients from the conception of their business ideas to full realisation through her pioneering incubation process, helping them transform purpose into profit and live balanced, fulfilling lives. Michelle's resilience and impact have earned her a commendation from the late Her Majesty Queen Elizabeth and the title of 'The Book & Business Midwife.' Her voice and story resonate globally, making her a sought-after speaker.

Through seminars, masterclasses, and programmes, Michelle equips individuals to pursue personal, financial, and entrepreneurial aspirations. Her passion is to help them shatter glass ceilings, embrace their true identity, and rise boldly into purpose and prosperity.

For more information about Michelle and her programs visit:
www.michellewatson.biz

Facebook
https://www.facebook.com/
IamMichelleWatson

LinkedIn
https://www.linkedin.com/in/
iammichellewatson/

Instagram
https://www.instagram.com/
iammichellewatson

Chapter Ten

EQUIPPED TO

Reign

How to Become the Woman Who Leads, Loves, and Liberates Through Christ's Power in You.

From Shame to Purpose

Have you ever felt like you didn't belong or that you had nothing of value to offer the world? Maybe you've even questioned whether life would be better without you. I have.

At 12, 24, and even at 30. Growing up, I felt like an outcast because I didn't look like those around me, I struggled in school due to undiagnosed dyslexia, and I often carried perspectives that set me apart. Instead of seeing those differences as strengths, I saw them as reasons I didn't measure up.

Although I grew up in a Christian household, it was not one filled with hope. My mom raised us as best as she could, but my early picture of God was one of stern judgment, not a loving relationship. I thought He only noticed me because Jesus died for my sins, not because He cared about me personally.

I worked hard to keep God happy. I tried to read the Bible daily, but it felt daunting. I envisioned God yelling at me. Shame became my shadow. I tried hard to be perfect, thinking that maybe then God and people would accept me.

But God in His mercy began peeling away those false layers. He revealed Himself not only as the King of Kings, but also as a Father and a Friend; One who delights in me, equips me, and wants me to thrive.

Discovering the Father's Heart

In my 20s, as I sought Him more deeply, God highlighted scriptures like:

"Ask, and it will be given to you; seek, and you will find; knock, and it will be opened to you. For everyone who asks receives, and the one who seeks finds, and to the one who knocks it will be opened." Matthew 7:7–8 ESV

Or "Which one of you, if his son asks him for bread, will give him a stone? Or if he asks for a fish, will give him a serpent? If you then, who are evil, know how to give good gifts to your children, how much more will your Father who is in heaven give good things to those who ask him! Matthew 7:7–11, ESV

Slowly, He showed me that my value isn't in being flawless, but in being His. He doesn't need me to have it all together before He can use me; He meets me right where I am and empowers me to grow.

That's when I began to understand: to reign as a woman of God doesn't mean striving for perfection; it means yielding to Christ's power in me. His strength enables me to lead with wisdom, love with compassion, and liberate others by sharing the freedom I've found in Him.

Reigning in My Unique Gifts

Romans 12:4-8 reminds us:

"For as in one body we have many members, and the members do not all have the same function, so we, though many, are one body in Christ, and individually members one of another. Having gifts that differ according to the grace given to us, let us use them: if prophecy, in proportion to our faith; if service, in our serving; the one who teaches, in his teaching; the one who exhorts, in his exhortation; the one who contributes, in generosity; the one who leads, with zeal; the one who does acts of mercy, with cheerfulness." (ESV)

I began to realize that what made me different wasn't a curse; it was a calling.

My dyslexia, once a source of shame, became a revelation. Research shows that nearly 35% of entrepreneurs are dyslexic; wired to see the world differently, solve problems creatively, and lead movements with vision others often miss.

Instead of viewing it as a limitation, I started to see it as God's design for my assignment. It became clear that He was equipping me not just to survive, but to reign; using my story, my voice, and my gifts to help others heal.

Building a Global Movement

Out of that revelation, God birthed something in me. I saw women trying to put themselves in a box. It's not good.

I believe women are overwhelmed by societal standards, feeling pressured to have it all together. As a result, they neglect their own needs, leading to health issues like autoimmune diseases. But it doesn't have to be that way. By empowering women to embrace their authentic selves and prioritize self-care, they can show up stronger for everyone around them.

Having gone through this myself and speaking to hundreds of women with similar experiences, I knew I had to act.

That's why I'm building a global movement where women feel supported to be authentically themselves. I do this by empowering and inspiring women with mentorship and training, helping them to confidently embrace their authentic selves and step into who they are.

The Blueprint for Reigning

Let's look at Proverbs 31:10-20 ESV:

An excellent wife who can find?
   She is far more precious than jewels.
The heart of her husband trusts in her,
   and he will have no lack of gain.
She does him good, and not harm,
   all the days of her life.
She seeks wool and flax,
   and works with willing hands.
She is like the ships of the merchant;
   she brings her food from afar.
She rises while it is yet night
   and provides food for her household

and portions for her maidens.

She considers a field and buys it;

with the fruit of her hands she plants a vineyard.

She dresses herself[e] with strength

and makes her arms strong.

She perceives that her merchandise is profitable.

Her lamp does not go out at night.

She puts her hands to the distaff,

and her hands hold the spindle.

She opens her hand to the poor

and reaches out her hands to the needy.

The Proverbs 31 woman became my blueprint; not because she was flawless, but because she ruled her domain with strength, vision, and love. She was entrepreneurial, nurturing, and generous. Her example shows us that leadership, business, and family life can all glorify God when we lean on His wisdom.

Like her, you and I are equipped to reign. Whether you are building a ministry, own a law firm, sell essential oils, or serve as a life coach, God has called you to this path for a purpose. I understand that the journey of entrepreneurship and ministry can feel lonely, especially as a Christian. My journey has taken years, and throughout it, fellow Christian sisters have often asked why I want to be a business owner. They've said, "You should use your gifts to glorify God, not for business."

Each time I heard that, I felt shame and confusion, because ever since I was a little girl, I felt drawn to entrepreneurship. But when God calls you to reign, it may not look like what tradition expects. No matter the form it takes, it always means walking in your God-given authority, influencing your sphere with love, stewarding your gifts faithfully, and ultimately pointing people back to Christ.

10 Practical Keys to Help You Reign with Holy Spirit Power

Before I close the chapter, I want to leave you with some practical tips to help you as you go into the next chapter of your business or ministry. Take some time now to dream with God and journal your thoughts on each point:

1. If you have a dream in your heart, God put it there for a reason. Ask what He wants you to do with it.

2. If you feel unqualified, I want you to think about all the people that God used in the Bible. God used Moses, who had a stutter, to speak up to Pharaoh and ask him to set his people free. God used Esther, an orphan, to set her people free from annihilation. Finally, God used me: someone who's dyslexic, to write this chapter for you. So, when you feel like you're unqualified, think about these people.

3. If you find yourself comparing your gift to those around you, remember God gave you the dream and vision for a reason. I always say comparison is the biggest joy stealer. You may have seen the images of a crayon and a pencil next to each other. Saddened, the crayon thinks to himself, "Wow, the pencil is so tall and sharp." The pencil thinks to himself, "Wow, the crayon is so colourful." Both of these writing tools are missing the amazing gifts they have to offer. The same goes for you. Don't compare your gifts to others and put yourself down. God gave you something special, and He wants you to use your gifts.

4. Remember, faith without works is dead, so as you take this next step of your journey, whether you want to change jobs, scale your ministry, start a new business, or enhance your current venture, you have to show God that you're ready by taking action. Miracles won't fall in your lap with you sitting there thinking about it and twiddling your thumbs.

5. As you think about the next chapter of your business, believe that you're worthy of it, and I want you to believe that it can happen, because belief is at the root of everything. God wants to do big things for you, and He will guide you every step of the way.

6. Watch your words. Words have power, and scripture says that life and death are in the power of the tongue. That's not only for how you speak to others but also for how you speak to yourself and over your business.

7. Apply the SMART acronym to the next chapter of your career, business, or ministry.

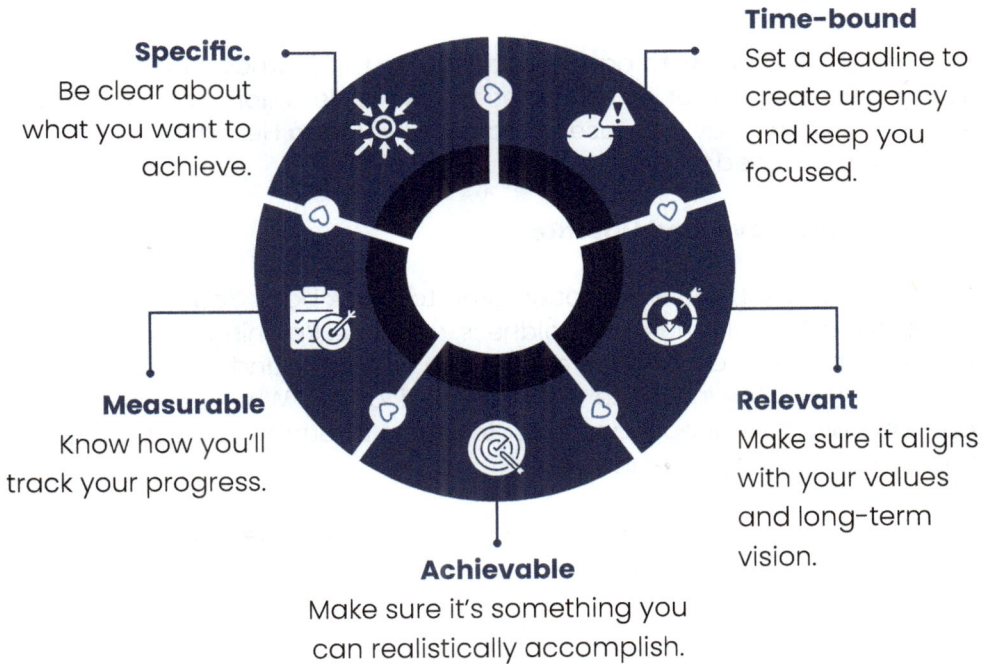

Specific.
Be clear about what you want to achieve.

Time-bound
Set a deadline to create urgency and keep you focused.

Measurable
Know how you'll track your progress.

Relevant
Make sure it aligns with your values and long-term vision.

Achievable
Make sure it's something you can realistically accomplish.

8. Surround yourself with people who have the same mindset as you. Studies show that you are the average of the five people you hang out with the most, so make sure that you're surrounding yourself with people who are going to take you closer to your goal, as opposed to those who will drive you away from it.

9. Find someone who's five steps ahead of you and have a conversation on their keys to success. Ask them for their advice and to pick their brain. They can give you insight into how they got there and pitfalls to avoid along the way.

10. Take time to reflect at the end of each week or month and think about how far God has brought you. Something I do at the end of each month is look through my photo album on my phone to review all the blessings God bestowed on me that month. This serves as a reminder that God has done great things for you, and it will give you hope that He will continue showing up.

Over the next week, I invite you to take a few minutes to write down one of the tips above and meditate on it. Then create an action plan.

Remember God wants to partner with you on this journey, and it's not your job to bring any of it to completion; it's His. He is going to carry you every step of the way because He cares for you and He wants to see you succeed.

A Call to Lead, Love, and Liberate

My beautiful sister, you were not created to shrink back. You were created to reign with humility, boldness, and love. Reigning looks like breaking free from shame, embracing your gifts, and stepping confidently into the influence God designed for you. When you lead authentically, love deeply, and liberate others through your testimony, you reflect Christ's power in you.

Before I leave you, here is a prayer to help you lead, love, and liberate through Christ's power in you.

A Prayer to Reign with Love

Dear God,
Show me the depth of Your love and remind me that I am equipped to reign. Reveal the unique gifts You've given me and give me the courage to use them with confidence. Help me release the pressure to be perfect and instead embrace Your strength in my weakness.

Guide me as I lead, fill me with love that overflows, and anoint me to bring freedom to others. Remind me daily that I am not overlooked or disqualified but chosen and empowered.

May my life be a reflection of Your kingdom:
strong, compassionate, and fruitful.

In Jesus' name, Amen.

A scripture for you to meditate on:

"And I am sure of this, that He who began a good work in you will bring it to completion at the day of Jesus Christ." Philippians 1:6 (ESV)

Some worship music to help you fuel your faith:

- Never Lost *by Elevation Worship*

- Every Little Thing *by Hillsong Young & Free*

- I Will Follow Jesus *by Circuit Riders*

- I'll Give Thanks *by Housefires*

About Angel:

Angel Theodore is a passionate Speaker, International Author, Certified Life Coach, and Founder of My Self-Care Catalyst, a global movement dedicated to empowering women to prioritize their well-being and embrace their authentic selves. Angel's work has been featured in USA Today, NBC, and Business Innovator Magazine.

Having personally struggled with her own burnout in 2019 and to keep up with societal pressures, Angel understands what women face and is committed to helping them heal. Her books, which include devotionals and journals, have been sold internationally, reaching women across the globe.

These powerful resources offer actionable guidance on self-care, self-love, healing, and prioritizing mental wellness.

Through her writing, speaking, and courses, Angel creates a safe space where women can reclaim their confidence, embrace their true selves, and thrive without performance. Her work continues to inspire and uplift women in a way that creates a lasting impact that extends far beyond borders.

For more information about Angel and the programs she offers through My Self-Care Catalyst, visit her website, connect with her through the outlets below, or scan the QR code for quick access.

Website
www.MySelfcareCatalyst.com

References

Logan, J. 2009. Dyslexic entrepreneurs: the incidence, their coping strategies and their business skills. Dyslexia, 15(4), pp. 328-346.

Rohn, J. (attributed). Quoted in: Canfield, J. & Switzer, J. 2005. The Success Principles. William Morrow.

Chapter Eleven

COMMISSIONED

*And
Unstoppable*

How to step out as a Kingdom Catalyst, World-Changer and Daughter on Divine Mission.

> *"They tried to bury us, but they did not realize we are seeds." - Poet Dinos Christiano Poulos*

Life is a journey filled with valleys and mountaintops, seasons of joy and seasons of challenge. As women, we often carry the weight of expectations, responsibilities, and the pressures of division and conflict. Some of us have faced deception in our faith and civil and religious leaders, rejection, oppression, loneliness, isolation, or the fear of speaking up. Others have experienced physical or emotional abuse, trauma, poverty, separation from family, community, or even from themselves. But here is the truth: nothing can separate us from the love of God (Romans 8:38-39).

Even when the world tries to bury us in doubt, struggle, distraction, division, or opposition, we are like seeds planted to grow, to flourish, and to bear fruit. Psalm 121 reminds us that God is our keeper, our protector, and the One who watches over our every step.

Psalm 121 The Lord My Guardian (The Holy Bible)

A song of ascents.
I raise my eyes toward the mountains.
From where will my help come from?
My help comes from the Lord,
the maker of heaven and earth.
God will not let your foot slip;
your guardian does not sleep.
Truly, the guardian of Israel
never slumbers nor sleeps.

The Lord is your guardian;
the Lord is your shade at your right hand.
By day the sun cannot harm you,
nor the moon by night.
The Lord will guard you from all evil.
He will always guard your life.
The Lord will guard your coming and going
both now and forever.

Faith is not just something we believe; it is something we live.

Are you ready to step into the fullness of your faith? Let us begin.

Trusting God's Vision for Your Life

When you create a dream board or set intentions for the day, you are not just setting goals - you are aligning your desires with God's greater purpose for your life.

Proverbs 16:3 reminds us, *"entrust your works to the Lord, and your plans will succeed."*

Trust that the dreams placed in your heart are not random; they are part of a divine blueprint designed for your growth, impact, and fulfilment. As you visualize your aspirations, invite God into the process. Seek His wisdom, lean on His promises, and remain open to His timing. Do you have a spirituality and career section on your dream board? On mine, I committed to be faithful to God until death. I also devote 15 minutes to prayer every day (of course I do more than that and I am called to do even more), as the world needs our prayers more than ever before.

What is your non-negotiable faith action?
Having a faith-related non-negotiable activity such as daily prayer, weekly worship, or regular scripture study anchors your life in purpose and consistency. In a world that is constantly shifting and filled with distractions, this sacred routine acts as a steady compass, reminding you of your core beliefs and values.

It nurtures spiritual growth, strengthens resilience during difficult times, and fosters a deeper connection with God and community. By setting aside time that is protected and non-negotiable, you communicate to yourself and to those around you that your relationship with the divine is a top priority, shaping how you make decisions, relate to others, and stay grounded in hope and gratitude. Attending Sunday in-person mass is one of my non-negotiables with online participation as needed. My first ask to the case manager upon my arrival as a refugee in the USA in 2009 was connecting me to the church.

If you don't have a non-negotiable faith action yet, invite Holy Spirit to join you in showing you what yours can be.

Embrace Where You Are Meant to Be

Life's journey is often unpredictable, leading us through seasons of joy, sorrow, separation, and reunification. Yet, every step is divinely orchestrated. When we feel displaced or forgotten, we must remember that we are exactly where God intends us to be. As women, we often wrestle with the pressure to conform. But God calls us to stand firm, to bloom where we are planted, and to trust His timing. You are not abandoned, you are positioned.

The Separation Could Not Separate Us

Surrendering my family and the loss of my career to God played a crucial role in my successful integration in the USA. Rather than dwelling on mourning the loss of my mother's homeland and the material belongings I had invested in for many years, I chose to embrace the opportunities of a new one. Based on my professional background and limited-people's perceived opportunities, I received many recommendations to move to other parts of the country, and I always questioned why God sent me to Tennessee. Even though the beginnings of my integration were not easy, I decided to trust God and the process, investing in building relationships and personal development (leadership, speaking, storytelling and coaching). That investment led to having a global audience as a speaker.

My story of resilience and courage touched many souls and reconnected to the world through my writings, attending conferences and making incredible new friends from different countries. At one point when I was told several times that I was overqualified for many jobs, I kept digging deeper about God's calling and I am confident that I landed my plane. I am letting God lead me and use me where he needs me.

Separation can be painful, especially from loved ones. My journey of physical separation from my children and eventual reunification with my family after two years taught me that though we may be physically apart, nothing can separate us from the love of God (Romans 9:38-39). Distance does not diminish our bond with Christ or with one another when we remain rooted in faith. Even when life scatters us, we are still connected with divine purpose. Like seeds planted in different fields, we grow and flourish in the places God has assigned to us. Also remember to wisely use the Armor God provided to you. My tradition of carrying the Bible on my trips saved my life.

The Role of Sisterhood in Times of Adversity

Women thrive in sisterhood. When one sister falls, another one lifts her up. Sisterhood is a survival strategy. The Bible is filled with stories of women who supported each other, like Ruth and Naomi, Mary and Elizabeth, Deborah, and Jael.

God designed us to stand together, not alone. We need each other. When fear whispers that you are unworthy, remember: You have a voice. You have a purpose. I praise God for giving me a warrior biological sister who battled and fought for me with God when everyone else was full of fear. I never doubted her love for me and my children when I was forced to be separated from them because of oppression. I often hear stories of siblings not talking to each other. If you are reading this book and that is your case, take courage to send love and pray for your sibling right now. You will see God glorify himself in a way you could have never imagined. In practicing forgiveness, I have learned to separate people from their behaviours. How about you?

Play Time: Shining Your Light
Pause for a moment. Reflect and journal on how you let your light shine in different areas of your life: How are you going to shine your light differently from now on? Faith is not passive, it is active!

Home: Do you have a prayer routine? Do you pray together as a couple/family? Do you share the scriptures? I once heard a preacher saying that if couples do not pray together, they do not stay together. If you are reading this message and prayer is not part of your daily routine, I would recommend re-evaluating and adopting a prayer habit. God asks us to pray without ceasing. 1 Thessalonians 17.

Backyard/Community: How do you extend God's love to your neighbours? Do you belong to a faith-based/inspired organisation? Where do you volunteer? Do you attend a bible study? If not yet, what could you do differently?

City/State/Province/Globally: How are you living out your faith beyond your immediate surroundings? Do you speak out when you see injustice?

The Importance of Community in Faith

No great mission in Scripture was accomplished by one person alone. Even Jesus surrounded Himself with disciples. Isolation weakens, but community strengthens. What does Jesus say about community? In Matthew 18:20, He assures us, "For where two or three gather in my name, there am I in the midst of them." God created us for relationships, to uplift and strengthen one another in our spiritual journeys. Being part of a Christian community is a great lifestyle.

Whatever journey you are on, be it leadership, entrepreneurship, ministry, career, or personal growth, know that success is built in the community. That's why I am on a mission to help overwhelmed faith-inspired entrepreneurs to start and scale their business with team mentality through the Faith-IN-Action Program.

I have friends who tell me that they have felt disheartened by the actions of certain faith leaders and believers who do not live up to the teachings they preach. Remember that we are all sinners and through our faith and prayers mountains are moved. It is good to have a spiritual home.

Yet, I understand that sometimes Christians struggle with worship styles different from those in their home countries or cultures. My encouragement is this: seek nourishment in multiple ways. If you find in-person worship challenging, make a suggestion to leaders and supplement it with online services. At my church we have masses in English, Latin, Swahili, and Spanish.

Jesus desires that more churches be opened, not closed.
Proverbs 13:22 reminds us of the lasting impact of legacy: "A good man leaves an inheritance to his children's children." In The 21 Irrefutable Laws of Leadership, John Maxwell calls this The Law of Legacy - teaching that a leader's lasting value is measured by succession.

This truth challenges us with three important questions:

- What will people say at your funeral?

- More importantly, what will Jesus say on your last day as a Christian leader in whatever role of leadership you are in?

- How are you preparing the youth around you to be empathetic leaders and how do you welcome new neighbours/comers? Sadly, I have seen and heard news about churches being sold or closing their doors-both in America and across Europe. This raises a vital question: Do we still need churches?

My answer is a resounding yes. We need more churches because more people need to know Jesus - or to come back to Him. The real question is: Are you helping your congregation or church to grow and sustain that growth?

I have seen so many churches with Christian schools and others with Language learning programs. Several churches have programs for young families, and these initiatives are encouraging and can be duplicated. The newcomers in our communities deserve to be treated with respect (Exodus 23:9). Collaboratively, we as Christians and Christian organisations must increase our actions to attract the abundance promised by God and fight the scarcity mindset.

This isn't only up to the leaders of the church. It's up to you and me too. One of the greatest challenges today is isolation among Christian entrepreneurs, within churches, and in other faith-based organisations. Yet God's desire is that we live and work together in unity, just like the early church (Acts 4:32). Many of our brothers and sisters also struggle with generational trauma and poverty.

By leveraging the diverse gifts within the body of Christ, and by truly knowing and supporting each other, we can break these cycles and build thriving communities.

This is how we can ensure that our churches not only survive, but flourish, leaving a legacy that will impact future generations to come.

Your calling is to live your faith and not to fake it.

The King of kings has commissioned you unstoppable, so it's now time for you to go shine and flourish in your community like other warrior women in the Bible: Ruth, Esther, Debra and Rahab to name a few.
You must remind your sisters that no matter what situation they are in, God Emmanuel is always on their side.

And remember, even if some circumstances made you feel that you were buried, you now know that you weren't buried... you were planted. Therefore, go and plant new seeds in new communities, collaborate and celebrate each other, break bread together, and spread the good news!

Here is a prayer to help you become unstoppable on your divine mission:

Heavenly Father, I praise you for your mission, protection, and provision.
You said that you watch over me and will not let me slumber.
You also said, "Ask and it shall be given."

Lord, I know your promises are always good.

Thank you for equipping me with your wisdom and the tools to accompany me on my unstoppable personal, professional and spiritual journey moving forward. I invite You to be the source, the center and CEO of every activity in my mind, body, soul, home, and all the communities where you need me most.

Heal all my traumas and alleviate any obstacles that will distract me from your mission.

Lord, forgive all my inequities. I pray for every life I touch, every household, and city I will visit, every gathering I attend and true fellowships I will co-create with you.

God, stay with me and preserve me from evil.

In Your almighty and precious name Lord Jesus I pray. Amen.

A scripture for you to meditate on:

"Without faith it is impossible to please Him for He that comes to God must believe that He exists and that He is a rewarder of those who diligently seek Him." Hebrews 11:6

Some worship music to help you feel unstoppable:

- Rain Down *by Jamie Cortez*

- Be Still My Soul (In You I rest) *by Kari Jobe*

- I am the bread of Life *by Suzanne Toolan*

- All Things Are Possible *by Hillsong Worship*

About Drocella:

Drocella Mugorewera is a four-times bestselling author, global speaker and visionary community builder. Born into a family of nine children, she earned a scholarship to study at the National University in Kyiv, Ukraine. Returning to Rwanda, she served as a member of Parliament and the government. In 2008, when her safety was threatened, Drocella fled alone to the U.S., courageously rebuilding her life in Tennessee with no money or family.

Her resilience and leadership earned her recognition as Executive Director of Bridge Refugee Services and as a Champion for Change award recipient. Today, Drocella is the Founder of a global movement supporting Christian women entrepreneurs and faith-based organisations to overcome loneliness and isolation by building flourishing communities. Could you be the next one?

For more information about Drocella and her programs visit:
www.Care4Eachother.com

Facebook
www.facebook.com/drocella.mugorewera.1

LinkedIn
www.linkedin.com/in/drocellamugorewera

Instagram
www.instagram.com/drocella_mugorewera

Invitation

You are invited...

This is just the beginning.

What you are holding in your hands is not only a book, but also a spark. It is part of a movement of women around the world who are being awakened to their God-given calling.

That's why we invite you to become a partner of the Kingdom Women Catalysts Ministry. As a partner, you join a global family of women committed to building businesses, ministries, and communities.

Together, we are answering the call to partner with 100,000 women leaders globally, and we would love for you to be one of them.

Your partnership doesn't just strengthen this ministry; it ripples outward to impact the world. Every book sold, every event hosted, every retreat run, and every seed sown helps us fuel women with faith, equip them with tools, and release them into their Kingdom assignments. And through our partnership with Global Renewal.

This is not about one ministry. It's about revival. It's about women awakening to who they are and boldly advancing God's Kingdom together.

If your heart is stirring as you read this, it's because you're already part of this story. We invite you to stand with us, partner with us, and walk this mission shoulder to shoulder. You are awakened. Now it's time to awaken others.

For more information about becoming a partner of this ministry, visit:
www.ChristianBusinessResources.com

www.ingramcontent.com/pod-product-compliance
Lightning Source LLC
Chambersburg PA
CBHW070046100426
42740CB00013B/2823